mixed metal jewelry workshop

mixed metal jewelry workshop

combining sheet
clay
mesh
wire
& more

mary hettmansperger

LARK
BOOKS

A Division of Sterling Publishing Co., Inc.
New York / London

Senior Editor: **MARTHE LE VAN**

Assistant Editor: **GAVIN R. YOUNG**

Art Director: **MEGAN KIRBY**

Photography Director: **DANA IRWIN**

Junior Designer: **CAROL MORSE**

Illustrator: **MARY HETTMANSPERGER**

Photographers: **STEWART O'SHIELDS AND STEVE MANN**

Cover Designer: **CHRIS BRYANT**

Library of Congress Cataloging-in-Publication Data

Hettmansperger, Mary.
   Mixed metal jewelry workshop : combining sheet, clay, mesh, wire & more / Mary Hettmansperger. -- 1st ed.
      p. cm.
   Includes index.
   ISBN 978-1-60059-515-8 (hc-plc : alk. paper)
   1. Jewelry making. I. Title.
   TT212.H4625 2010
   739.27--dc22
                                    2009030530

10 9 8 7 6 5 4 3 2 1

First Edition

Published by Lark Books, A Division of
Sterling Publishing Co., Inc.
387 Park Avenue South, New York, NY 10016

Text © 2010, Mary Hettmansperger
Photography © 2010, Lark Books, a Division of Sterling Publishing Co., Inc.
Illustrations © 2010, Lark Books, a Division of Sterling Publishing Co., Inc.

Distributed in Canada by Sterling Publishing,
c/o Canadian Manda Group, 165 Dufferin Street
Toronto, Ontario, Canada M6K 3H6

Distributed in the United Kingdom by GMC Distribution Services,
Castle Place, 166 High Street, Lewes, East Sussex, England BN7 1XU

Distributed in Australia by Capricorn Link (Australia) Pty Ltd.,
P.O. Box 704, Windsor, NSW 2756 Australia

If you have questions or comments about this book, please contact:
Lark Books, 67 Broadway, Asheville, NC 28801
828-253-0467

Manufactured in China

ISBN 13: 978-1-60059-515-8

For information about custom editions, special sales, premium and corporate purchases, please contact Sterling Special Sales Department at 800-805-5489 or specialsales@sterlingpub.com.

For information about desk and examination copies available to college and university professors, requests must be submitted to academic@larkbooks.com. Our complete policy can be found at www.larkbooks.com

dedication

This book is dedicated to my son Logan. Thank you for being who you are.
I am proud to have you for a son and blessed to have you in my life. I love you.

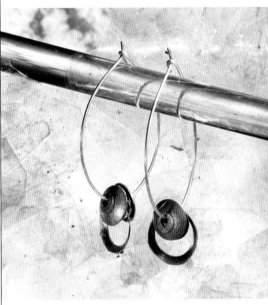

mixed metal jewelry
contents

introduction

There's nothing like watching the transformation of clay into shiny wearable jewels. When I was introduced to the exciting world of silver, bronze, and copper metal clays, I found that many techniques I already used in jewelry construction were complemented by them. Clay also allowed me the freedom to sculpt, mold, and twist any design I could imagine. When the soft material was in my hands, I realized the endless possibilities for combining it with sheet metal, wire, mesh, beads, and other objects. It became one of my favorite artistic endeavors, and I'm thrilled to share my journey with you.

To begin our workshop, you'll learn the basics of sheet metal and metal clay, including information about the materials and tools required, firing schedules, and several wire working and cold connection techniques. From there, you'll begin to understand the joy of creating a comfortable work space that prepares you for an inspirational, productive, and safe design experience. And then the journey begins!

You'll transition into making fabulous jewelry that covers the gamut from rings and necklaces to bracelets and brooches. The first five designs focus only on sheet metal. It's nice to get your feet wet before easing into clay work and combining materials. You'll use a variety of techniques that reappear in the three subsequent clay sections, and you'll tap into the sheer fun of jewelry design. Some of the skills and applications are extremely basic and are considered non-traditional in metalsmith work, but you'll soon realize they have endless possibilities for developing your own ideas and designs.

The next three sections of the workshop spotlight a variety of metal clays— silver, bronze, and copper—all accompanied by five projects. As you progress through the book, you'll begin to notice that each clay has its own special charm. For instance, silver clay naturally lends itself to layering, entwining, weaving, and folding. The Interweave Pendant (page 81) is an excellent example. Bronze clay gets two thumbs up for color. Beautiful patinas offer an element of surprise and adventure to each design. With copper clay, you'll find that it adheres to itself extremely well as you roll beads for the Draped Copper Trio (page 118). Not to mention, copper looks absolutely beautiful with other metals, particularly silver.

There's no denying how much you'll love your new handmade rings, bracelets, pendants, and brooches. Be warned: your friends will want them! But during this workshop, you'll also truly enjoy getting to know the distinctive characteristics of the clays and their individual personalities. The material gives designers a new opportunity to create fresh, exciting works of art that are stylish, timeless, and tailored to their exact taste. Now, channel your inner artist, and let's get busy.

materials

SHEET METAL

The projects in this book feature copper, silver, and brass sheet. I use 24-gauge copper and brass sheets for their versatility. When working with sterling silver, I use the thinnest sheets possible to cut down on cost. The most economical choices are usually 24-, 28-, and 30-gauge sheets. When layering sterling silver sheet over another metal, the thinner 30-gauge silver sheet can be used without compromising the strength of the jewelry.

Sheet metal

copper

Copper sheet, mesh, and foil are some of my favorite materials for making all styles of jewelry. In addition to its pleasing aesthetic quality, copper is also inexpensive and readily available. In this book you'll use copper in a variety of applications and find that the material is suitable for many uses. For example, copper is a perfect visual complement to silver clay, and it holds up well to silver clay's firing schedule.

When copper is heated with a torch, colors will appear on its surface. The colors will range from yellows and pinks to dark purples, reds, and oranges. These shades are much more vibrant than the look of aged copper.

All copper develops firescale when fired in a kiln. Firescale is a black carbon that looks like soot or dirt on the copper. To reduce this, I remove the metal pieces from the kiln while they're hot and quench them in cold water. This process causes the firescale to pop off the surface. Kiln-fired copper develops a reddish patina or a rustic dark surface. If you don't like these qualities, you can use a bench grinder with a de-burring wheel, a brass brush, or a polishing attachment on a rotary tool to buff the copper's surface back to a shine. Over time, the shine will disappear and the copper will turn a deep, dark color. I love the rich quality of the copper as it ages.

copper sheet

Copper sheet can easily be drilled, cut into a variety of shapes, textured, and forged. I use 24-gauge copper sheet for all of the projects in this book because, at this thickness, it is rigid but easy to cut. Also, 24-gauge sheets perform extremely well in the kiln with silver clay. There are numerous decorative applications for copper sheet, such as forging the edges with a hammer to give them a deckled appearance and creating interesting surface textures and effects with the rolling mill and other tools such as awls, files, and metal brushes. Copper is also my favorite metal surface on which to apply patinas. Heat patinas offer a wide range of colors and effects. Liver of sulfur turns copper black very rapidly. To avoid too much exposure, apply the liver of sulfur to the copper, and then immediately wipe it off. To create an antique appearance, I put a minimal amount of solution on the textured areas of the metal, and then buff the piece back to a shine.

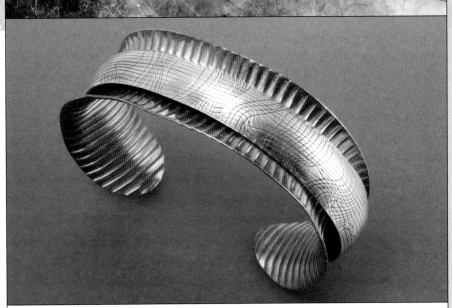

Cindy Pankopf *Anticlastic, Synclastic* 2009
2.2 x 7.5 x 5 cm, copper sheet, sterling silver sheet; microfolded, roller printed, formed
Photo by artist

copper foil

Copper foil is a thin metal sheet ranging from 0.002 to 0.006 inch (0.05 to 0.15 mm) thick. I enjoy working with the thinnest variety due to its versatility. It's available from metal or jewelry suppliers and is also stocked at some craft and hardware stores. Copper foil is extremely easy to use and manipulate—perfect for weaving, framing, and backing projects. Copper foil can be cut with scissors or folded and bent with needle-nose pliers. If you want to patina the copper foil, make sure it doesn't have a tarnish prohibitor on its surface. If it does, you can burn it off with a torch, but always work outdoors or in a well-ventilated area. Also, be aware that the edges and corners of copper foil can be sharp. Copper foil can't be fired in a kiln. It disintegrates at high temperatures.

Copper foil

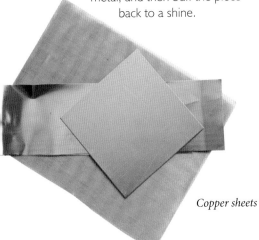

Copper sheets

silver sheet

Silver sheet is used in a variety of ways throughout the book. I use dead-soft sterling silver sheet because it is easy to work with. My preferred thickness for layering, small projects, folds, and wraps is 30-gauge. It's soft to work with, and once forged and work-hardened, it becomes a nice strong piece of silver. I also use 24-gauge sterling silver sheet for a few of the projects because of its added weight and strength.

You can heat silver sheet to create texture, but you must do so carefully. This process is called reticulation. A propane torch with ambient air is not quite hot enough to reticulate silver, but a propane torch mixed with oxygen produces a hotter flame and will work. It is possible to create heat patinas on silver. The color variations are different than on copper, leaning more toward gold, yellows, browns, and purples.

metal mesh & screen

Screen and mesh are made of woven wire. The most common types of wire used to make screen and mesh are copper, stainless steel, and brass. These products are usually found through metal suppliers or at hardware stores. Galvanized hardware cloth is easy to find at home and garden or hardware stores, and comes in several sizes.

I love using woven metal products with metal clay because they present a world of possibilities and produce amazing results. Embed mesh and screen into metal clay to create interesting surfaces. Press the clay through woven wire. This particular process extrudes the clay through the weave and creates a nice textural element that can be added to jewelry.

When galvanized cloth is used with metal clay, the shrinkage of the clay is much more noticeable. The clay pulls away from the cloth, creating holes and gaps. I find galvanized metal cloth especially appealing when used with bronze clay.

Stainless steel mesh is beautiful to use when making silver jewelry. Due to the stiff quality of the material, I recommend using a fine grade of stainless steel mesh, such as one that measures 160 x 160 per 1 inch (2.5 cm). This is the perfect size to bend, cut, and manipulate. It fires beautifully with silver clay.

It's important to remember that metal clay shrinks when fired and will therefore adhere to woven materials. Make certain to securely attach the clay and the woven material, either through embedding or creating a clay bezel that will grab and hold the screens when fired.

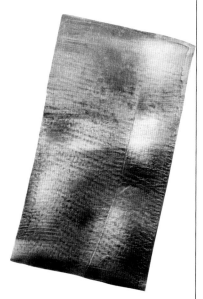

Silver sheet

*Screen &
metal mesh*

WIRE

Because of its pliable nature, wire can be used in a variety of jewelry-making applications. It can add detail, function, and interest to jewelry designs. Wire is a fantastic material for making connections. The gauge of wire indicates its thickness—the smaller the gauge number, the thicker the wire. Thin 26- and 24-gauge wires are good for weaving and stitching, while sturdier 22-, 20-, and 18-gauge wires work well for spokes, hangers, and other structural jewelry components.

An array of patinas can be applied to both copper and silver wire. Liver of sulfur and heat patinas are the coloring methods I use to darken or age wire. Thick wires can be forged with a hammer to flatten their shapes or flare their ends. If you apply heat to the end of copper or sterling silver wire, the end becomes molten and forms a ball. Purchase copper, tin-coated, and brass wire from metal or jewelry suppliers or at some home supply and hardware stores. Silver and silver-plated wire is sold primarily through jewelry suppliers. Colored and craft wire is available at most craft supply stores.

silver & copper wire

Silver wire is a beautiful material that's worth the extra expense. Silver wire is sold in three degrees of malleability: hard, half hard, and soft. Hard wire is more difficult to work with but holds its shape once formed. Half-hard wire is easier to work and has a nice rigidity. Soft wire is very flexible and easy to manipulate. Beginning jewelers will find

Becky I. Chader *Arizona Collar: A Wearable Reliquary for Sharp Pointy Things* 2007
38.8 x 3.5 x 1.5 cm, sterling silver, red brass, peridot, cactus prickers, plunger clasp; fabricated, cast, pierced, slot and tab constructed, cain making, set
Photo by artist

silver wire more difficult to manipulate, weave, and handle than copper wire because it's less flexible. When learning a new technique, I recommend trying it first with copper or a plated wire before using silver.

Copper wire is very pliable and easy to use. Make sure to purchase bare wire that doesn't have a protective coating or tarnish inhibitor. The aged or tarnished look that develops over time is a nice look on copper. You can speed up this process by using a heat or liver of sulfur patina. Copper wire that is 22-gauge or thicker fires well with metal clay.

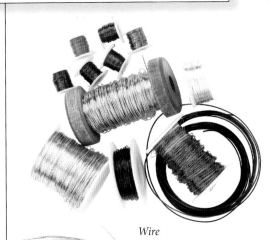

Wire

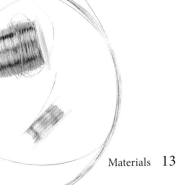

Melissa Muir Untitled 2008
6 x 5.2 x 0.5 cm, sterling silver, copper, rubber; formed, fabricated, forged, pierced
Photo by artist

Silver-plated wire

Colored wire

tin-coated & silver-plated copper wire

Silver-plated copper wire is a little more expensive than tin-coated copper wire, but it is my favorite inexpensive wire with which to learn and practice new skills and designs. Tin-coated copper wire has several drawbacks. It's not as shiny as silver; it has a tendency to darken the skin; and its ends do not ball as nicely when heated. However, its aged effect and duller gray color works well with found objects, and it is a very nice alternative to more expensive wires. Working with tin-coated copper wire is relatively easy, similar to working with copper.

colored wire

There is a wide variety of high-quality colored wire being produced. This material will add color, texture, and interest to your jewelry. Use small-gauge colored wire for weaving, stitching, and wrapping applications. Larger-gauge wires can be fun in wrapped loops, bails, and other accents. The colored wire that has a copper base is the best quality. Color-coated base-metal wire is less useful. Coated wires do have their drawbacks. Over time, most will lose their coating from wear and none should be heated with a torch. If you notice the colored finish of craft wire flaking, don't use it.

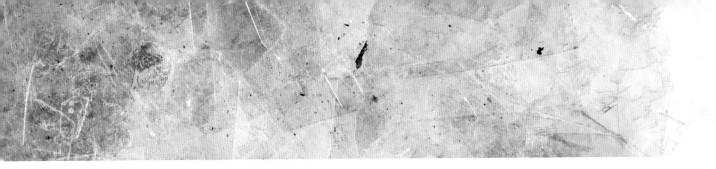

METAL CLAY

Metal clay has changed the way many jewelers and craftspeople approach making metal jewelry. This relatively new material has many possibilities. Metal clay is made up of small particles of fine silver, gold, bronze, or copper suspended in water and a binder. Once fired by a torch or in a kiln, the water and binder burn away, leaving only the metal.

silver clay

Silver clay is manufactured in several forms, including lump, paste, syringe, and sheet. As the formula of silver clay has been refined, there is less shrinkage during firing. This makes the clay a wonderful material for what I like to do best: mix metals.

silver lump clay

Several types of metal clay are produced, and each offers the jewelry artist different qualities that are beneficial in different situations. The first generation of metal clay had 28% shrinkage rate and fired at 1650°F (900°C). Newer clays have a 12% shrinkage rate and fire in less time and at a lower temperature. The type of clay I prefer fires at 1400 to 1472°F (760 to 800°C) for 30 minutes or can also fire at 1600°F (871.1°C) for 30 minutes to give it added strength. I prefer firing this type of clay in a kiln rather than with a torch. Especially when mixing the clay with other metals, I have found that a kiln fires the clay at a more constant temperature than a torch.

Metal clay

metal clay paste & slip

Metal clay paste and slip can be described as watered down versions of lump clay. Both are applied with a soft-bristle paintbrush. These materials are used in a similar fashion to ceramic slip, as a glue to connect dry metal clay pieces. Paste and slip are invaluable when designing slab constructed objects or hollow forms. You can make your own paste out of metal clay dust and small scraps, so always save your leftovers.

Metal clay paste, slip & sheet

syringe clay

Applying metal clay with a syringe allows for precision and accuracy. I like to use syringe clay in combination with lump clay to create surface textures and make connections and repairs. Several different tip sizes for the syringe are available, giving you many options for extruding the clay.

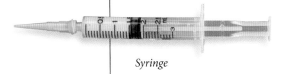

Syringe

Davide Bigazzi *Autunno Cuff* 2003
3.8 x 7.6 x 0.6 cm, sterling silver, copper, bronze; hand fabricated, repoussé
Photo by AZAD

Silver clay

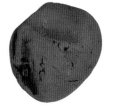

Bronze clay

Copper clay

metal clay sheet

Metal clay sheet is a paper-like version of silver clay that is pliable and easy to use as a surface embellishment. Sheet clay is a fascinating form that is easy to manipulate. It's very flexible and has been designed to remain moist, allowing for a longer working time than lump clay. Sheet clay folds and bends without breaking, making it perfect for weaving projects. Be careful not to add too much water to the sheet. It will literally fall apart if it gets too much moisture. Many jewelers work the sheet clay while it's dry, folding it like origami.

recommended firing schedule for silver clay

Firing times and temperatures vary by manufacturer and product. Always check the packaging on your metal clay and follow the manufacturer's directions for firing time and temperature. For the projects in this book, unless otherwise mentioned, I prefer clay that fires at 1400 to 1472°F (800°C) for 30 minutes or can also fire at 1600°F (871.1°C) for 30 minutes to give more strength.

bronze clay

Much like silver clay, bronze clay is composed of metal particles suspended in water and a binder. Bronze clay consists of 11% tin, 89% copper, water and nontoxic binding materials. The binding materials completely vaporize during the firing process, leaving a solid bronze piece. Bronze clay is beautiful and more affordable than silver clay. The most notable difference is the length of the firing time.

Bronze clay requires a slow kiln schedule to ramp up the heat, and then must be held at that temperature for a longer period of time. Bronze clay also needs to be fired in a stainless steel container surrounded in an activated carbon, to reduce oxidation. Due to this lengthy firing schedule, bronze clay is not as instantly gratifying as silver clay, but the pieces that can be created with it are stunning. Straight out of the kiln, the color of the bronze surface is gorgeous. You can leave the kiln patina or polish the fired piece to a high shine. Both surfaces have great creative potential.

recommended firing schedule for bronze clay

Ramp the kiln at 250°F (139°C) per hour until it reaches 1550°F (843°C). Hold the kiln at this temperature for three hours. The total firing time, including ramp time, will be approximately nine hours. (Firing times and temperatures vary by manufacturer and product. Always check the packaging on your metal clay and follow the manufacturer's directions for firing time and temperature.)

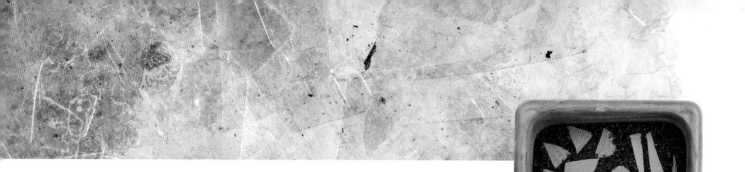

copper clay

Copper clay consists of pure copper, water, and nontoxic binding materials. Copper clay is a great new product. It's moist, making it easy to manipulate; its firing schedule is shorter than bronze clay; and it's less expensive than silver clay. Since I'm so fond of copper sheet, this new clay has been a wonderful material to work with. Its deep blue, yellow, dark rust, and brown colorations straight out of the kiln are amazing, and I also love it polished to a high shine. Like bronze clay, copper clay must be fired inside a stainless steel container surrounded by carbon, but it is fired for less time than bronze clay. Important: Do not fire copper clay in coal-based carbon because the piece will not sinter. Instead, use coconut carbon to assure the sintering.

recommended firing schedule for copper clay

Ramp the kiln at full speed to 1700°F (927°C) and hold it at that temperature for three hours. The total firing time for copper clay, including ramp time, is approximately four hours. (Firing times and temperatures vary by manufacturer and product. Always check the packaging on your metal clay and follow the manufacturer's directions for firing time and temperature.)

activated carbon

Activated carbon helps prevent oxygen from interfering with bronze and copper clay's sintering process. In metallurgy, to sinter means to form a solid mass by heating a material without melting it. The clay pieces must be positioned inside a lidded stainless steel container and surrounded by one of the activated carbons when fired to reduce oxidation. There are two types of activated carbon, one is coconut-shell based and works with copper clay, while one is coal based and works with bronze clay. To keep matters simple, I keep both carbons on hand but in separate stainless steel containers.

coconut carbon

Coconut-shell based carbon is the best variety in which to fire copper clay and yields the best colorations. Coal based carbon will not sinter copper correctly and can cause breakage. Coconut carbon can be used repeatedly to fire copper clay.

activated coal carbon

Use coal based, acid-washed carbon when you fire bronze clay. The material will sinter properly and the fired pieces will achieve a beautiful color. Coal based carbon can also be used repeatedly to fire bronze clay.

Activated carbon

Coconut carbon

Coal carbon

Kathy Williams *African Ladies* 2008
6.5 x 3.5 x 3 cm, sterling silver, copper, garnets, amber, glass beads, patina;
fold formed, hydraulic pressed, altered, fabricated, pierced, riveted, cast, sandblasted
Photo by Stephen Funk

Glue & fixative

arranging metal clay in activated carbon

1. Layer the activated carbon, approximately ½ to 1 inch (1.3 to 2.5 cm) thick, on the bottom of the stainless steel container.

2. Arrange the metal clay pieces on the carbon, leaving a ½-inch (1.3 cm) space between larger pieces. (Smaller pieces can be placed closer together.) Keep all pieces from ½ to 1 inch (1.3 to 2.5 cm) inside the edges of the container.

3. Sprinkle the activated carbon on top of the first layer of metal clay pieces approximately ½ inch (1.3 cm) thick. Continue in the same manner, placing layers of unfired metal clay and layers of activated carbon in the stainless steel container.

4. Always finish with a layer of activated carbon as the top layer, leaving enough room for the lid to fit on the container and lay flat.

GLUES & FIXATIVES

A high quality, two-part epoxy can be useful on occasion to hold materials in place, such as dried wood in the Catch & Pendant on page 77. You can also glue pin backs in place instead of soldering them if desired.

Spraying a very light coat of fixative over a patina can help adhere and preserve the colored surface. I rarely use a fixative. I prefer letting the surfaces of my jewelry age naturally and take on richer, darker patinas. When using any glue or fixative, make sure to work in a very well-ventilated area or outdoors, as some of these products are harmful to inhale.

low-temperature tube solder

Low-temperature tube solders bond metal when heated with the most basic propane torch. The product is quick and simple to use and works with most forms of metal, including metal clay. I use low-temperature solder with brass, copper, and silver.

low-temperature soldering —adhering a pin back

1. Determine where the pin back should be located on the back of the brooch.

2. Clean the area with a scouring cleanser or pickle solution.

3. Use the syringe to place the paste solder in the desired location.

4. Position the pin back on the line of solder, making sure there are no gaps between the metals.

5. Gently and gradually heat the area with the torch. Be careful not to place the flame too close to the brooch.

6. Watch for the solder to become liquid and flow. Once this happens, the surfaces will be adhered.

7. Let the brooch air cool or spritz water on the heated area to cool it more rapidly.

COMPONENTS & CONNECTORS

Commercial components and connectors can be any manufactured item that suits your fancy. Scour through bins at a hardware store, and let your imagination roam. Electronic salvage stores are an amazing resource, offering small metal parts at a very low cost. Scrapbook stores have loads of metal items that can be used as cold connections. Many readily available, unconventional supplies can be adapted into jewelry. Coins, sticks, washers, and discs are non-traditional objects that make a nice impact on metal jewelry. Always keep a lookout at craft and beading supply stores, fabric stores, flea markets, scrap metal yards, and antique stores—just to name a few!

nuts and bolts

Use small nuts, bolts, and rivets from the local hardware store to connect layers of metal sheeting. Miniature nuts and bolts can be ordered through eyeglass repair suppliers, electronic retailers, and hobby stores, as well as jewelry suppliers. Small brass, stainless steel, and copper varieties are readily found. Just before making a nut-and-bolt connection, I place a drop of glue on the threads of the nut to ensure the bolt will not unscrew over time. To connect metal sheets with a rivet, hammer the backside of the rivet to spread out the metal. This creates a lip that secures the rivet in place.

Low-temperature tube solder

Components, connectors & found objects

eyelets & rivets

Eyelets and rivets can be used to connect two pieces of metal or strictly for embellishment and surface design. These small pieces of tube have a rolled edge or lip on one end that, when secured, leaves the hole in the metal exposed. Eyelets are easy to set with a simple tool. Commercial rivets are generally solid rather than hollow and are used in the same manner as eyelets. Do not place eyelets or rivets into a kiln; they are not designed to withstand extreme temperatures.

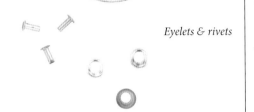

Eyelets & rivets

setting an eyelet

Make setting eyelets one of the last steps in constructing a jewelry piece so as not to damage the eyelet. For detailed information on setting particular eyelets, follow the manufacturer's instructions.

1. Feed the eyelet through the hole with the large rimmed end on the front of the piece.

2. Place the eyelet tool on the opposite, smaller end of the eyelet on the backside of the piece.

3. Hammer the tool to spread out the tube, securing the eyelet in place.

scrapbook supplies

I've found scrapbooking stores to be a great resource for jewelry supplies. Eyelets and brads are sold in a broad range of colors and metals. You can also purchase mica in ready-to-use sheets. Base metal and copper charms and ephemera of all shapes and sizes can be great jewelry embellishments.

EMBELLISHMENTS & EPHEMERA
beads

Beads should come with a warning label—the more you have, the more you want. Whether enhancing a connection or dangling from a head pin, beads are fantastic jewelry embellishments. Beads come in a wide range of materials, colors, designs, sizes, and finishes, and shopping for them at specialty stores is delightful. Most beads are measured in millimeters, with the size referring to the bead's diameter. When you're considering beads for a project, make certain that their holes are large enough to accommodate the thickness of the wire you intend to use. I especially enjoy hunting for and using metal beads in my jewelry. You can also create unique handmade beads with metal clay. In the techniques section on pages 53 through 55 you'll learn how to form and texture flat disks, rolled beads, and hollow spheres.

Beads

Robert Longyear *Yesterday's Attire #11* 2006
9 x 9 x 4 cm, iron wire, sterling silver, concrete; fabricated
Photo by Don Casper

found objects

Found objects—anything from antique coins to bus tokens to bottle caps—can add visual interest to jewelry and make pieces truly one-of-a-kind. Layer them with traditional materials to make unique designs. In the Currency Pendant on page 71, I capture a coin, making it into a reversible necklace. Bottle caps or lids can be used in the same way for a whole different look. In Catch & Keep Pendant (page 77), the spotlight is on organic sticks captured in metal. You can successfully incorporate found objects by making them an intricate part of a design. Changing their shape, surface, or function always makes a found object more interesting. By using found or unconventional items in your jewelry, you remove them from their regular context and imbue them with entirely new and different meanings.

I use many types of bottle caps in my jewelry designs. Rusted caps provide an interesting surface texture, but they need to be cleaned with soap, water, and a wire brush to remove any rust particles from the surface before using. Always wear a dust mask to avoid inhaling rust particles. After the cleaned caps are dry, apply non-yellowing, matte fixative to the surface. Once dry, test the sealed finish by rubbing it with a clean white cloth.

mica

Mica is a natural material that is semi-translucent, often with an amber or tan coloration. It can be purchased at craft supply and scrapbooking stores. Because mica has a tendency to flake and peel, make sure to layer it between two layers of a sturdier material, such as metal, to help protect it from becoming damaged.

Mica

Lori McCoy Bellamy *Cherry Blossom Necklace* 2007
18 x 14 x 1.5 cm, sterling silver, copper; forged, fabricated
Photo by Hap Sakwa

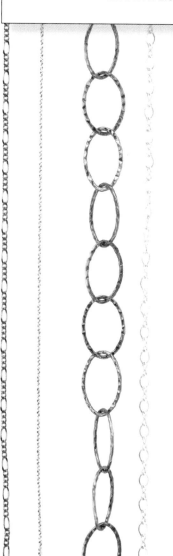

JEWELRY FINDINGS

Jewelry findings make a piece of jewelry wearable. Pin backs, stickpins, neck chains, clasps, toggles, bails, and ear wires are just some examples. Commercial findings are sold in a variety of metals, from 14-karat gold and sterling silver to hypoallergenic base metals. They also come in a wide range of styles, from ornate filigree work to modern minimalism. Select a finding design and a metal type to suit the piece of jewelry you make. Keep in mind that some alloys can tarnish and dull over time and often darken the skin. Some people are allergic to base metals, especially ear wires. Buying precious metal findings is often well worth the extra cost.

neck chains

Choose commercial neck chains to fit the style of a piece of jewelry, both in length and in appearance. In most cases, I prefer using sterling silver chain. Because you'll be working with mixed metals in this book, your selection of neck chains is very broad. If a silver or copper chain is too bright and shiny to suit the antique patina of a pendant, darken the chain with liver of sulfur. Pre-oxidized sterling silver chains are another option. They often complement the aged look of bronze and copper. Purchasing chain by the foot (30.5 cm) is slightly less expensive than purchasing ready-to-wear chains, and it allows you to create a neck chain of any length. Clasps are purchased separately and added by hand, making unusual necklace lengths easy to achieve. You can also purchase ready-to-wear neck chains with clasps in standard lengths.

I tend to use standard length chains, frequently 20 and 24 inches (50.8 and 61 cm) long. I also like choker-style wires and cables for pendants that hang close to the neck. This short length keeps the pendant from moving as freely as it would on a longer chain. Making your own neck cord out of waxed linen is another option. Braid, crochet, or half-hitch 4-ply waxed linen cords to create a wonderful woven look.

irish waxed linen, elastic & neck cords

Although I string many jewelry pieces on ribbon, leather, and hemp cords, waxed linen is my favorite. It is a strong and reliable material that performs well as a neck cord. Waxed linen comes in a wide range of colors and various ply options. I prefer four-ply waxed linen because it is sturdy yet easy to work. It can be purchased from basketry, bead, and bookbinding suppliers. If you can't find waxed linen in a store, try shop-

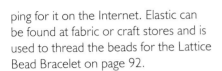

ping for it on the Internet. Elastic can be found at fabric or craft stores and is used to thread the beads for the Lattice Bead Bracelet on page 92.

jump rings

Jump rings are small wire circles used to connect jewelry components. Although you can purchase premade jump rings in many metal types and with different diameters and wire thicknesses, it is simple (and economical) to make your own. Each jump ring has a slit that is opened with pliers. Jewelry elements are fed onto the ring through its slit, and then the ring is closed. I often use several jump rings at once to form a connection and avoid any one ring being under too much pressure. Jump rings made from heavier gauge wire are less likely to open with wear and tear. You can also solder your jump rings closed for a more secure connection.

clasps

Once you have chosen a chain, you'll likely need to add a clasp to make a necklace or bracelet wearable and secure.

Spring-ring clasps are made of a ring with a small lever that, when pulled back, opens the clasp. A link of chain is fed through the ring and when the lever is released, the chain is secure. Spring-ring clasps are quite common, function well on many pieces, and are sold in precious and base metal varieties.

A toggle clasp is a two-part design. One part of the toggle is a bar shape and the other part is a loop. One component is attached to each end of the bracelet or necklace. The bar-shaped component is fed through the loop-shaped component and turned crosswise to secure. Commercial toggle clasps are available in a variety of patterns and designs and in many types of metal.

ear wires

Ear wires attach to earrings to make them wearable. Commercial varieties are available, but you can easily bend your own. Half-hard silver wire is a good choice for sturdy ear wires. You can use soft sterling silver, but be sure to lightly hammer the ear wire once it's shaped to work harden the metal. Use sterling silver or a hypoallergenic metal to prevent allergic reactions to ear wires. Copper ear wires look great, but not everyone can wear them.

pin backs

Commercial pin backs feature a rectangular piece of flat metal that you attach to the back of a brooch, most often by soldering. A long, sharpened wire stem rises from the metal to pierce the clothing. The point of the stem fits into a clasp that secures it in place. Some styles of pin backs have three holes in the flat metal rectangle. These holes make it possible to sew the bar to the back of a brooch.

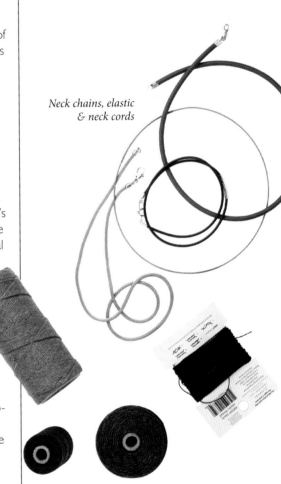

Jump rings, clasps & pin backs

Neck chains, elastic & neck cords

studio space

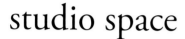

As an artist for more than 25 years, I have learned to maintain a balance between home life and having a successful career. Creativity is often a tough process to tap into, and distractions only make it harder. Having a studio, no matter where it is or how big, is an important consideration.

I've had my workspace or studio in a variety of places, knowing I would ultimately try to build a space to fit my needs. I've worked almost everywhere—in my lap, at the kitchen table, during baseball games, in my basement, and even at a luxurious downtown loft. I'm fortunate that some of my artwork allows me the freedom to pick it up and work anywhere. Other efforts have fixed locations due to the equipment I use. This variety gives me changes of scenery and stimuli as I work.

Much like my artwork, my studio has evolved. In every case, changing spaces, moving, and growing has brought new adventures, excitement, and challenges. I strongly feel that my studio has had an impact on my artwork, work habits, and success as an artist. If you are in it for life, a studio must be a priority. You have to be content and open to work in the space you choose.

DEDICATING A SPACE

Of course, we all dream of working in a place that is spacious, functional, and easy to organize, but no matter where you are or how much space you have, I believe that the approach should be the same. Your first task is to designate a specific area to be your studio. This space does not have to be elaborate or vast, but does need a few important amenities. The foremost requirement is to make sure it has is a good "vibe." You must be able to create in the environment and this sense is personal to each artist. Whether you like a space that's quiet or filled with music, one that's chock full of visual stimuli or beautifully sparse, your studio needs to fulfill your personal affinities so you will be open and free to create.

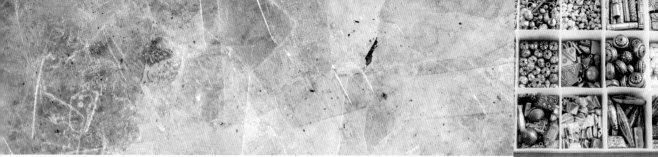

SUSTAINING A HEALTHY ENVIRONMENT

There are many studio requirements specific to metalwork. First and foremost is setting up and maintaining a healthy work environment. You must setup and adhere to safety precautions when working with an open flame and chemical fumes. Good ventilation is critical. Avoid working in tight enclosed areas that have no options for letting in outside air or properly filtering it. I use an exhaust fan to maintain the flow of fresh air in my space. I also close off portions of the space so I don't lose heating or cooling in the entire studio. Whenever possible, circulate fresh air into the studio from outdoors. Opening several windows or a door will help to pull fumes out of your studio. When I am applying or burning any chemicals, I only work outside.

ARRANGING YOUR SUPPLIES & ARTWORK

Your workspace should also be a safe haven for tools, materials, and artwork. If you live and work with other people, all too often your tools become "community property" and end up missing. Nothing is more frustrating than having to hunt down your tools whenever you begin to work. Try to organize your tools so creating can happen easily. Materials and supplies need to be organized as well. When your tools and materials are well organized and accessible, you can turn your creativity loose. I've expanded my work area over the years, and with every move or major overhaul, I have improved my organization of the entire space.

I feel it's beneficial to display your jewelry, both pieces in progress and completed works. Revisiting a piece in the light of a new day allows you to critique your work more thoroughly. I also work on several pieces at once, letting different works inspire each other and me.

Organizational compartments

equipment
& tools

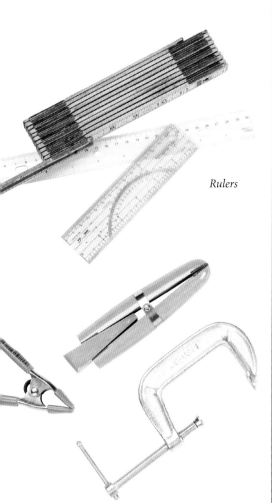

Rulers

Spring, ring & adjustable clamps

Kaylin Hertel Untitled 2006
20 x 16 x 1.5 cm, copper, nickel, patina; riveted, heat colored
Photo by Aaron Paden

GENERAL PURPOSE TOOLS

You'll use the following items for many projects, so keep them on hand.

rulers

Use a ruler to measure the dimensions of materials. Metric units are particularly easy to calculate and are useful for jewelry's small size.

adjustable, spring & ring clamps

Clamps come in very handy when working with metal. Use the adjustable clamp to secure work or tools to a table or bench. Some power tools have a tendency to crawl away from me as I work, so I use heavy-duty adjustable clamps to keep them in place. Spring clamps have rubber tips and can be purchased at a hardware or home supply store. I use spring clamps to hold jewelry parts together as I work or to secure metal pieces to the end of a table while I drill. Ring clamps have a soft grip of rubber or leather and are great for holding jewelry while you buff on the bench grinder. They are also excellent for securing work and act like a third hand. Purchase ring clamps from jewelry suppliers.

Metal sheet cutters & snips

TOOLS FOR CUTTING METAL

Shears and a jeweler's saw are the primary tools for cutting metal. Disk cutters can be used to make perfect circles of various dimensions. A simple flathead screwdriver will cut a rough opening inside a sheet of metal. If you have tools you prefer using and find helpful, feel free to use them in your work.

metal sheet cutters & snips

Metal sheet cutters have flat blades that are good for straight cuts or wide curves, and they leave a clean edge. The design of this tool has really improved over the years and there are many varieties from which to choose. This is one tool that is well worth a splurge. Buy the highest jewelers-quality sheet cutter you can afford. I use them to cut metal more frequently than I use a jeweler's saw.

disk cutter

A disk cutter is a useful tool that cuts a perfect circle out of metal. A set of disk cutters includes an assortment of cutters with graduated diameters. To use a disk cutter, place the sharp edge of the tool on the sheet metal and strike the other end of the tool with a hammer.

jeweler's saw & saw blades

To make my designs, a jeweler's saw is not a required tool. I like to cut metal with shears and cut holes with a sharpened screwdriver. However, many experienced jewelers feel more comfortable with a saw and like the clean edge that a saw creates. Either cutting method is fine to use for the projects in this book.

using a jeweler's saw

1. Secure the saw blade in the saw frame.

2. Attach a bench pin to your worktable or jeweler's bench.

3. Place the sheet metal on top of the bench pin.

4. Hold the blade at a 90° angle to the sheet metal.

5. Gently saw in short strokes to begin the cut. (Make sure you do not use too much pressure on the saw, as it is easy to break the fine jewelry blades.)

6. Lengthen your stroke and continue cutting the metal as desired.

Set of disk cutters

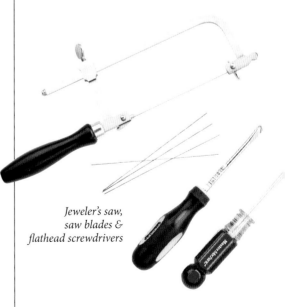

Jeweler's saw, saw blades & flathead screwdrivers

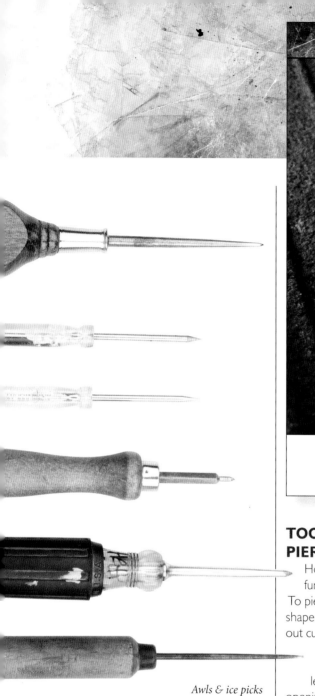

Awls & ice picks

TOOLS FOR PIERCING METAL

Holes in metal can be used for functional or decorative purposes. To pierce metal means to cut out a shape on the interior of the sheet without cutting its edge. A sharp pointed awl, ice pick, or flathead screwdriver will pierce a hole, but leaves the metal with an irregular opening. If precision piercing is desired, use a drill bit or hole punch. Purchase drills and drill accessories from jewelry suppliers, hardware stores, or home supply centers. Hole punches specifically made for metal are only available from jewelry suppliers. I prefer using a hole punch rather than a drill for fast projects. Always wear safety glasses, a dust mask, and gloves when you're drilling metal.

awl or ice pick

Awls and ice picks have a variety of uses. Prior to drilling metal sheet, use an awl to punch a pilot hole so the drill won't slip across the surface. Strike the top of the handle of an awl or ice pick with a hammer to punch a hole in metal. Create a dimpled texture (a series of small indentations) on sheet metal by gently hitting the top of an awl with a hammer. When using metal clay, I often use an awl to create a pilot hole in the wet clay. Later, on the dry or fired piece, I expand the pilot hole with a drill bit.

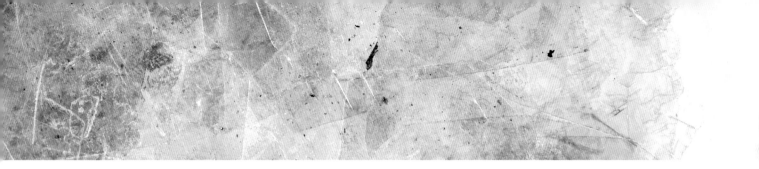

flathead screwdriver

I frequently use simple square- and triangle-shaped openings in my designs. As barbaric as this may seem, I've found that the sharpened tip of a flathead screwdriver is a great cutting device, and I use it instead of a jeweler's saw. I place the sharpened edge of the screwdriver where I want to cut the metal and hammer the end of the handle to cut the sheet. This method gives the interior "windows" in my jewelry an organic look.

hand drills

To make holes in metal, use a drill bit made for metal with a flexible shaft machine, a regular hand-held drill, or a drill press. The projects in this book feature many small holes used for eyelets, brads, stitching, and connections. All of these holes are a consistent 1/16 inch (1.6 mm) in diameter. If using small nuts and bolts, use a drill bit sized to match the bolt.

wood block

To protect your work surface from the drill bit, place a block of wood underneath the metal sheet. A block of hardwood, such as hickory or oak, will hold up longer than a soft wood. You can buy a wood block at a home supply store or use a scrap leftover from a woodworking project.

Flexible shaft machine

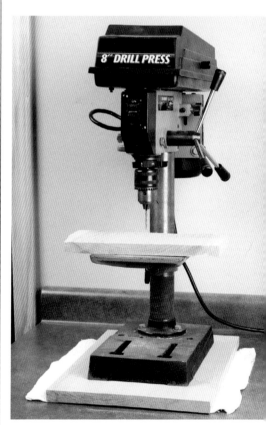

Drill press

Una Barrett *The Accountant's Daughter* 2009
2 x 17 x 1 cm, sterling silver, bronze, brass, 14-karat gold, garnet, citrine, smoky quartz, bone
Photo by Stewart Stokes

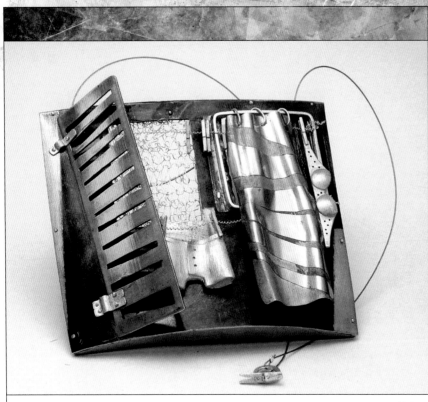

Elida Kemelman *Trapitos al sol - pendant* 2007
9 x 11 x 3 cm, sterling silver, nickel silver, bronze, copper; engraved
Photo by artist

sawing & piercing metal

1. Drill a small hole through the sheet metal.

2. Loosen one end of the saw blade from the saw frame.

3. Feed the free end of the saw blade through the drilled hole in the sheet metal.

4. Secure the blade back into the saw frame.

5. Saw out the interior shape, and then reverse the process to free the blade from the sheet metal.

TOOLS FOR WIRE WORKING

Whether you want to cut, bend, hold, or straighten wire, there's a tool designed for every need.

wire cutters

A wire cutter is an essential tool for cleanly cutting wire. They are available in a wide range of styles and prices and are sold at jewelry suppliers, home improvement centers, or hardware stores. For snipping lengths of wire, any type of cutter will do. However, when cutting wire to finish a piece of jewelry, I prefer to use jeweler's quality side cutters. This model snips wire as closely as possible and leaves the nicest end.

hole punches

A variety of punching tools will cut holes into sheet metal. My preference is a hand-held version that is operated much like a traditional paper punch. (Feed the flat metal sheet into the tool, and squeeze the handle.) This type of punch is available in several sizes that are equivalent to standard drill bit diameters, such as 1/16 inch (1.6 mm) and 1/8 inch (3 mm). Another style that is very popular is a small, screw hole punch with two size options. This tool looks similar to a helicopter with two metal bars at the top. Sheet metal is inserted into the bottom cutting area and the metal bars are turned to create the holes.

Hole punches

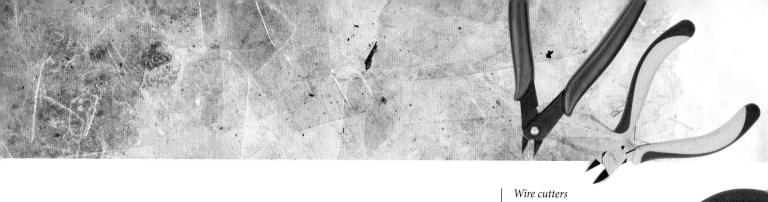

pliers

Pliers are used in a variety of ways, and therefore come in many shapes and sizes. For handling screen, mesh, copper foil, and wire, I use long, needle-nose pliers. These have a flat interior without any teeth or ridges and never leave unwanted marks. I use them for pulling wire, bending and shaping metals, and to hold metal in the flame. They often become my third hand. Round-nose pliers are great for making wrapped loops and for advanced wire-working techniques.

wire smoothing tool

This tool is designed to straighten and smooth wire that has curls or kinks. It's similar to a pair of pliers. The big difference is that thick, heavy, soft plastic covers the inside of the jaws on a wire smoothing tool. To use one, simply insert your wire into the jaws of the tool, firmly grip the end of the wire, pull to smooth, and repeat if necessary.

TOOLS FOR FORMING METAL

Metal can be formed in many ways, such as forging, texturing, stamping, and rolling through a mill. Here are descriptions of the forming tools used in this book.

hammers

Large heavy hammers are great for forging and aging metal sheet. Use small hammers to forge the ends of wire into paddle shapes and to create a variety of textures on metal surfaces. I use a ball-peen hammer to make small round indentations on sheet. Hammers are also used with awls and eyelet-setting tools. Jewelry suppliers sell a large assortment of hammers for specialized work, but I most often use a typical hardware-store variety.

anvil & steel block

An anvil and a steel block are two surfaces on top of which sheet metal is hammered to create texture and form. Small anvils or blocks are useful when you are working on small pieces. They are also portable. To buffer the noise anvils make when they are struck, you may wish to place yours on top of a sandbag, towel, or mouse pad. In my studio, I use a sturdy anvil and vise combination that I purchased from a hardware store. This type of vise/anvil combo can be securely attached directly to your workbench. The vise is a nice addition to my tools and comes in handy for holding head pins, bending metal, and as a third hand in certain applications.

Wire cutters

Pliers

Wire smoothing tools

Vise, hammers, & steel block

Dapping blocks & daps

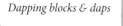

Catherine Butler *Marsh Moonrise* 2008
5.1 x 7.2 x 1.5 cm, brass, copper, sterling silver, patina; sawed, pierced, hammered, roller printed, soldered
Photo by Jordan Davis

Stamping tools

Ring mandrel

dapping block & daps

A dapping block is used with a dap and a hammer to shape sheet metal into domed shapes. The block is square with curved depressions on its surface. A corresponding dap fits into each circle in the block. To dome the metal, place a round disk into a depression in the block. Position the round end of the dap over the metal. Gently strike the flat end of the dap as often as needed to form the disk into a dome.

ring mandrel

A ring mandrel is a tapered metal cylinder used to determine ring measurements. Most are marked with incised lines that indicate different sizes.

stamping tools

You can use stamping tools on both sheet metal and metal clay products. They can be purchased individually or in sets of letters and designs. Metal letter sets are great for writing on jewelry and for "signing" jewelry with your initials. Always press stamping tools into metal clay before it's dry to make the indentation.

TOOLS FOR HEATING METAL

In this book, a propane torch is used to heat sheet metal, to burn wire ends into balls, and to patina copper surfaces. A kiln is used to fire metal clay. Before beginning to work with heat, review and become familiar with all the other tools and safety precautions (such as eye and hand protection) related to torch and kiln firing.

firebrick & tripod screen

Use firebricks to create a protective, heat-resistant surface for hot techniques. I suggest setting up a grid of firebrick close to torch and kiln areas. Because I use heat to patina so much copper, I've covered an entire table with firebrick outside my studio. Use a tripod screen for small soldering jobs and heat patinas. I always make sure I have the table surface covered with firebrick or a similar fire-resistant material.

propane torch

I used a small propane torch as the heat source for all the projects in this book. This simple torch produces a large flame that burns fairly clean and hot. The torch is fitted with a small canister of propane. There are several options for the tip of the torch. My favorite is the self-igniting variety because it doesn't require a striker. I use the standard tip that comes on the torch. It's the perfect size for the work that I do. (Smaller tips can create flames that are too intense for the materials used in this book's projects.) For simple connection jobs, such as attaching pin backs and soldering sheet metal on top of sheet metal, you can use low-fire solder with this torch. Purchase this type of propane torch and replacement tanks at home improvement and hardware stores.

Traditional metalsmiths most often use an acetylene torch because it burns hotter than a propane torch. The heat from this type of torch works well for all metal jewelry applications, including soldering, and can be used as the heat source for all the projects in this book.

Firebrick & tripod screen

Propane torches

Metal clay kiln

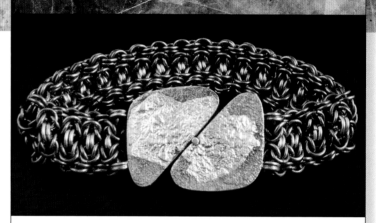

Fran Grinels *Gold Mine* 2008
3.8 x 17.8 x 0.6 cm, sterling silver, 24-karat gold, 22-karat gold,
18-karat gold; fabricated, kum boo, oxidized
Photo by Sam Grinels

Kiln shelves & furniture

Stainless steel container

metal clay kiln

A kiln is a type of oven traditionally used for firing ceramics and enamel, but it is also used to fire silver, bronze, and copper clay. Using a kiln is the best way that I have found to fire metal clay pieces. Silver clay can be torch fired, but is strongest when kiln fired. Bronze and copper clay can only be fired in the kiln.

A good kiln is an expensive piece of equipment, but given the time and investment that goes into jewelry making, it will pay for itself. I use a 110-volt kiln with a grounded plug. It came pre-programmed with five firing schedules, but I also have the option of setting my own. There is a window in my kiln door, which is an optional feature.

kiln shelves & furniture

Kiln shelves let you fire multiple layers of silver metal clay pieces at once. The "furniture" consists of stackable tables and legs. I usually place pieces of a shelf or a soldering pad on the bottom of the kiln and then stack furniture two layers high. This gives me a total of three layers for firing pieces.

stainless steel container

Bronze and copper clay must be fired inside a stainless steel container. The container sits on a kiln shelf and the stacked items must fit in the kiln. I recommend positioning the stainless steel container in the center of the kiln and elevating it on a low shelf so the heat remains as evenly distributed as possible on all sides of the container.

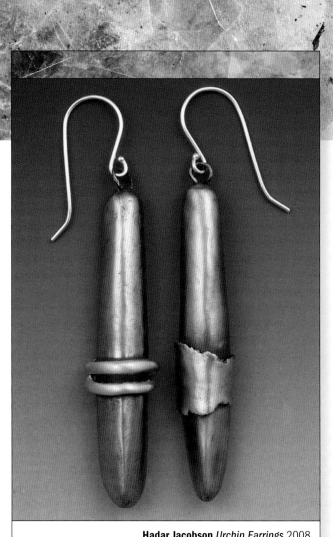

Hadar Jacobson *Urchin Earrings* 2008
4.5 x 0.5 x 0.5 cm, silver, bronze, and copper clay; kiln fired
Photo by artist

Kiln spatulas

Hot pads & firebrick

Bowl

spatula

A kiln spatula is specifically designed to retrieve hot items from the oven. As you pull items out of a kiln and transport them to be quenched, be sure to keep the spatula level. A hot item can easily slide off a tilted spatula.

safety gloves & hot pads

Wear a pair of heat-resistant gloves or heavy work gloves when taking items out of a hot kiln. Kiln heat is intense. Burns can happen very quickly and the hot temperatures can also dry your skin. You can also use hot pads to handle and transport items and hot containers. Lay hot pads and metals on firebrick to cool.

bowls

Keep one or two bowls of water near your torch and kiln so you can quench hot items. Sturdy and stable metal bowls make the best containers.

Sandpaper & scrub pads

Brass & metal brushes

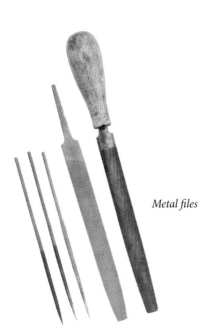

Metal files

TOOLS FOR FINISHING METAL

Use these tools during metal fabrication and to put the final touches on a completed jewelry piece. They can be used both for metal sheet and metal clay.

metal file

After cutting metal sheet into a desired shape, it's likely to have rough edges. Smooth the edges with a flat file, and then hammer them to eliminate any remaining irregularities. Always check to make sure the edges are becoming smooth and soft from filing, not sharp and dangerous. If you make clean cuts and forge correctly, you may not have to file your metal. Before using a file on metal clay, let it dry completely. Hold the dried clay and gently file it, without putting too much pressure or stress on the clay, or it will break.

brass or metal brush

A metal bristled brush is a great tool for adding matte surface textures to your jewelry. The brushes can also be used to cut through heavy patinas, reducing some of the applied color and bringing the original color of the metal back to the surface. A metal brush is also a good tool for buffing and polishing the fired metal clay.

sandpaper

In this book, sandpaper is primarily used on dry metal clay. I place the sandpaper face up on my work surface and gently pull the clay over the paper. This method lets me apply the right amount of pressure on the piece of clay, rather than pushing too hard and breaking it.

Lynn Cobb *Spinner Ring* 2009
2.6 x 2.6 x 2.6 cm, silver clay, 22-karat gold
Photo by George Post

Burnishing tools

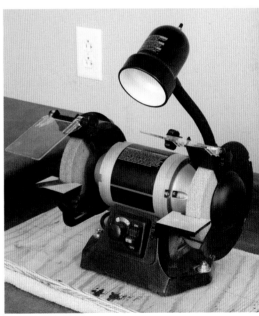

Bench grinder

burnishing tool

Use this tool to polish or burnish a metal surface. When used with force, a burnisher can create a near-mirror finish. This tool works well to polish raised areas on textured surfaces.

steel wool

Steel wool can be used to smooth and de-burr rough metal. You can also use it remove the shine from a metal surface, creating an attractive matte or scratched finish.

bench grinder

A bench grinder is one of my favorite tools by far. It has many uses, including sharpening cutters, de-burring sheet metal, and polishing metal sheet and clay. Always use this tool with extreme care and attention, and wear your safety glasses. Because of its high rotations per minute (RPM), the wheels on a bench grinder can grab items very fast.

Playing cards & slats

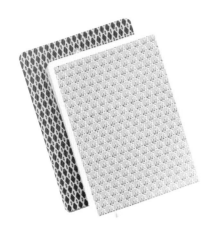

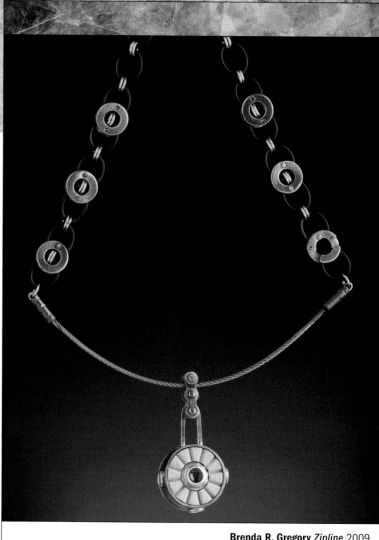

Brenda R. Gregory *Zipline* 2009
17 x 15.5 x 1 cm, stainless steel cable,
copper rivets, resin, rubber o-rings
Photo by Steven Gregory

eyelet tool

Eyelet tools are found at scrapbooking, craft, and discount stores. Follow the manufacturer's instructions to properly install eyelets. The process is very easy. It can be used to give a smooth lip to holes drilled in metal. Eyelet tools come in two common sizes: one for the larger ⅛-inch (3 mm) standard eyelet and one for the small 1⁄16-inch (1.6 mm) eyelet, often referred to as a mini eyelet.

TOOLS FOR METAL CLAY

Many tools have been designed to use specifically with metal clay, but many common craft supplies and household items also come in handy.

playing cards or slats

Often, you will want to roll out a sheet of metal clay to a specific thickness. Using equal stacks of traditional playing cards or plastic slats will help you maintain consistency.

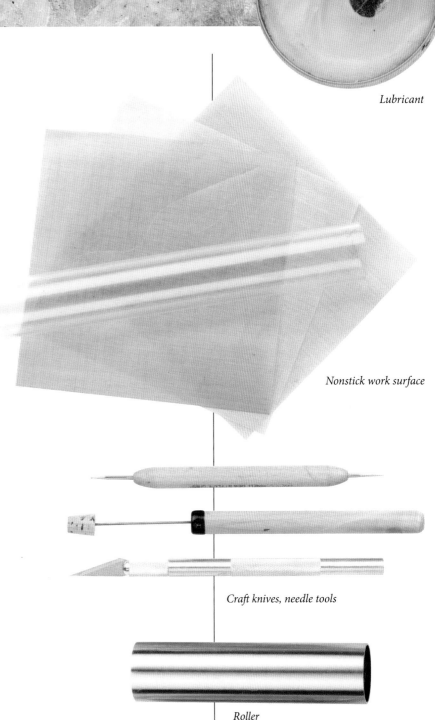

Lubricant

plastic or metal roller

Use a plastic or metal roller to form a lump of metal clay into a slab. This process is similar to rolling out pie dough. Be sure to start working with small lumps of metal clay until you develop a feel for the amount needed to make a slab.

lubricant

A lubricant is used to keep the metal clay from drying out and to keep it from sticking to your hands, roller, and work surface. Many people use pure olive oil, but I prefer the consistency of a thicker balm. Since I tend to be a messy worker, a more dense lubricant is easier to manage.

Nonstick work surface

craft knife

This sharp cutting instrument slices through metal clay cleanly. I use the tip of the knife to gently poke and thereby pick up very small metal clay pieces. You can also use a craft knife to make fine surface texture in metal clay.

nonstick work surface

There are several types of nonstick work surfaces available. Choose one that suits your working style and needs. Plastic or acrylic surfaces with grids or self-healing cutting can be used, or a rigid surface like glass is also a good choice. Flexible thin plastic cut into small squares is helpful when making individual projects.

Craft knives, needle tools

Roller

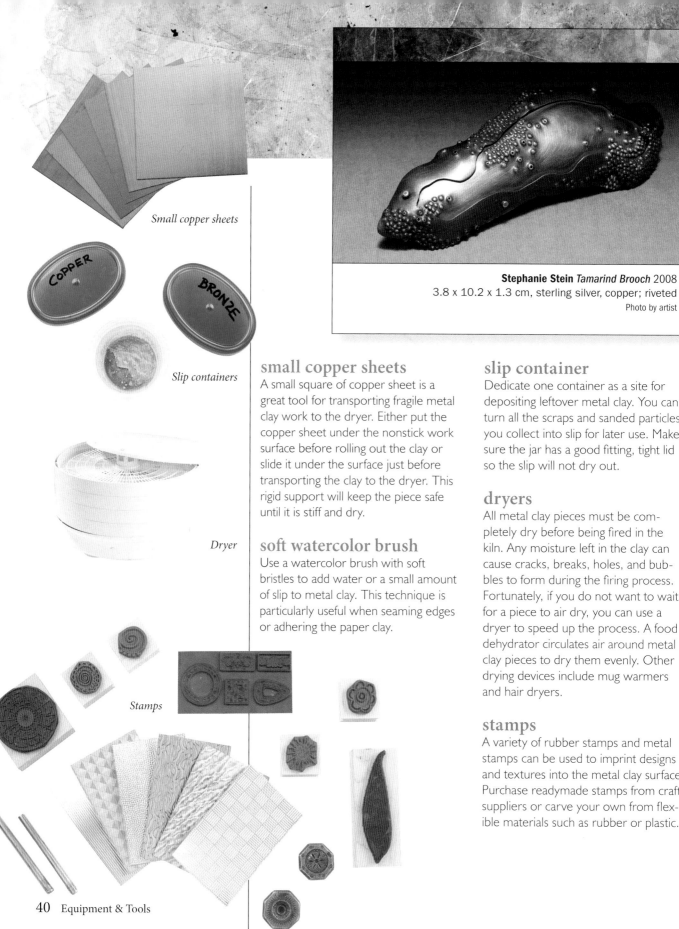

Small copper sheets

Slip containers

Dryer

Stamps

Stephanie Stein *Tamarind Brooch* 2008
3.8 x 10.2 x 1.3 cm, sterling silver, copper; riveted
Photo by artist

small copper sheets

A small square of copper sheet is a great tool for transporting fragile metal clay work to the dryer. Either put the copper sheet under the nonstick work surface before rolling out the clay or slide it under the surface just before transporting the clay to the dryer. This rigid support will keep the piece safe until it is stiff and dry.

soft watercolor brush

Use a watercolor brush with soft bristles to add water or a small amount of slip to metal clay. This technique is particularly useful when seaming edges or adhering the paper clay.

slip container

Dedicate one container as a site for depositing leftover metal clay. You can turn all the scraps and sanded particles you collect into slip for later use. Make sure the jar has a good fitting, tight lid so the slip will not dry out.

dryers

All metal clay pieces must be completely dry before being fired in the kiln. Any moisture left in the clay can cause cracks, breaks, holes, and bubbles to form during the firing process. Fortunately, if you do not want to wait for a piece to air dry, you can use a dryer to speed up the process. A food dehydrator circulates air around metal clay pieces to dry them evenly. Other drying devices include mug warmers and hair dryers.

stamps

A variety of rubber stamps and metal stamps can be used to imprint designs and textures into the metal clay surface. Purchase readymade stamps from craft suppliers or carve your own from flexible materials such as rubber or plastic.

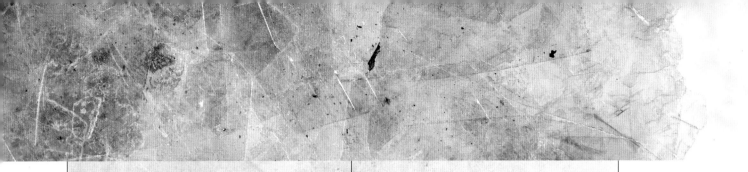

SHEET METAL KIT

Ball-peen hammer

Bench grinder

Bowl of water, iced or cold

Dapping block and daps

Disk cutter

Drill with $\frac{1}{16}$- and $\frac{1}{8}$-inch
(1.6 and 3 mm) bits, or $\frac{1}{16}$- and
$\frac{1}{8}$-inch (1.6 and 3 mm) hole punches,
or awl with sharp point

Measuring tape or ruler

Metal file

Metal snips

Needle-nose pliers

Old pliers

Propane torch

Round-nose pliers

Safety glasses

Safety gloves

Steel block or anvil

Wood block

METAL CLAY KIT

Bench grinder with burr wheel
(optional)

Bowl of water, iced or cold

Brass brush

Craft knife

Kiln

Measuring tape or ruler

Nonstick surface

Old pliers

Olive oil or lubricating balm

Paintbrush

Plastic or metal roller

Playing cards or plastic slats

Polish

Propane torch

Rubber stamps

Safety glasses

Safety gloves

Sandpaper

Straws, small and large

metal techniques

This chapter introduces you to how I use metals. I like to experiment with materials, techniques, and alternative applications. Being unconventional and fearless lets me be very creative. Since my background is as a fiber artist, my approach to designing and making jewelry is not traditional. For example, most jewelers try to avoid firescale at all costs, while I like using it as an unorthodox surface treatment. I often use low-tech connection methods such as stitching, weaving, and layering instead of soldering. I like the look of rustic metal, patinas that add depth and age, and texture, so I avoid the refined, smooth, and shiny finishes. The processes I cover in this chapter barely scratch the surface of metalworking, but there is plenty here to get you started making mixed metal jewelry.

1

WORKING WITH SHEET METAL

After years of weaving and connecting fibers and textiles, working with wire and sheet metal felt very foreign at first. The more I worked with metal, the more fascinating it became. Once annealed, sheet and wire becomes malleable, like fabric, and can be beautifully bent and shaped.

annealing

Working with metal hardens it by compacting its crystalline structure. Annealing (heating) work-hardened metal returns the crystalline structure to its original, softer state. This makes the metal easier to bend, cut, and manipulate and extends the time the metal can be worked without becoming brittle.

step by step

1 Hold the metal to be annealed in a pair of pliers with a protective handle.

2 Light the torch and hold the metal sheet approximately 1 inch (2.5 cm) away from the end of the torch tip. This positions the metal in the hottest part of the flame. If the metal is too close to the tip, you can actually snuff out the flame. If the metal is positioned too far from the tip, it won't get hot enough.

3 Heat the metal with the torch until it glows (photo 1). (If using the propane torch, the metal will reach this stage in just a minute or two.)

4 Remove the glowing metal from the flame and air-dry or quench it in a bowl of iced or very cold water.

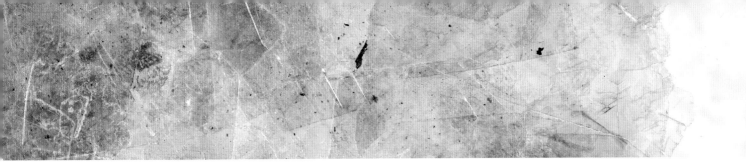

firescale

Firescale is an oxide that forms on the surface of heated metal. It is caused by oxygen combining with copper at high temperature. Firescale will form on copper and also on sterling silver due to its copper content. When jewelers solder metal, they first cover the surface with flux: a protective coating that prevents oxygen from reaching the surface when heated.

There are many ways to deal with firescale. Since my jewelry has an altered-art style, I prefer the rustic look that metal receives from firescale and heat patinas. But, if you wish to remove it, my favorite way is to buff it off with a bench grinder and a soft de-burring wheel. You can also remove firescale with a brass brush or file. Many metalsmiths use a warm pickle solution to clean and reduce oxides on their work. I rarely use pickle because I like the aged and rustic look I achieve by reheating metal instead of cleaning it. Reheating metal and quenching it in cold water reduces oxygen exposure and firescale and produces lovely coloration.

Kiln-fired silver clay does not produce any firescale, but kiln-fired copper sheeting does. To minimize firescale but still achieve remarkable patinas, move the hot, fired copper directly from the kiln to the cold-water bath. You'll be amazed at the red tones produced by quenching.

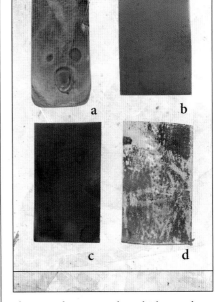

If a piece of copper reaches a high enough annealing temperature, then once quenched, the front surface (where the flame was) will turn a bright red color and the backside will turn black as shown in figures A and B. This red coloration is called a cold-water patina.

Whether it's air-dried or quenched, the annealed metal will become equally malleable, but I find that the cold-water quenching process better prepares the metal to take a patina.

After working the annealed metal, it will become hard again and the coloration that came from the initial annealing will change. The deep red color fades and the black is often hammered away. If you want the vibrant red to stay in the final piece, do all the hammering and texturing on the copper before heating it. Try hammering the dark backside (figure C) to achieve an antique look (figure D).

Firescaling

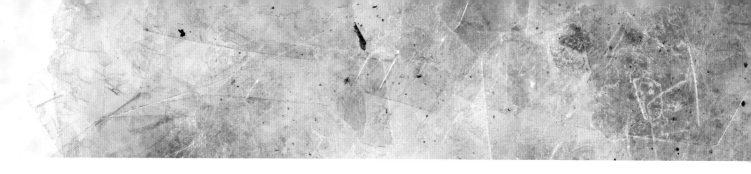

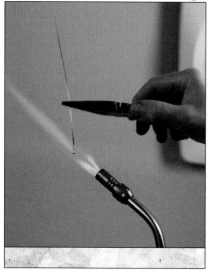

Copper wire can be held from the side or from the top of the flame. Balls will form on copper wire ends no matter the angle.

To create uniformly round balls, hold silver wire from the top of the flame. Silver has a tendency to slump to one side if it is not held from above the flame.

Always ball the ends of tin-coated wire under an exhaust fan or outdoors because dangerous fumes are released from the tin coating.

Putting copper wire in a kiln will soften it, but will not produce balled ends.

balling wire ends

You can finish the cut ends of copper or silver wire by heating them with a torch. The flame will cause the end of the wire to melt and form a ball. This is an attractive application and is used for many projects in this book.

Balling wire ends

step by step

1 Hold the length of wire in a pair of old pliers.

2 Light the torch and place the end of the wire in the flame, about 1 inch (2.5 cm) from the end of the tip and ½ to 1 inch (1.3 to 2.5 cm) inside the flame itself (photo 1).

3 Once a ball forms, gradually pull the wire out of the flame. (If it is removed too quickly, the ball may become distorted with a point on the end.) If left in the flame too long, the ball will become too large and drop off.

coloration

• If you remove copper wire from the flame at its melting point and put it directly into ice-cold water, it will develop a permanent bright red/pink patina.

• If balled copper wire is allowed to air-dry instead of being quenched, it will turn black.

• When you ball and quench sterling silver wire in cold water, the ends will turn pale pink.

• Fine silver wire with balled ends remains a bright silver color.

• The ends of tin-coated wire will turn red/bright pink like bare copper when balled.

1

Jason Morrissey *July 12 Bead* 2006
4 x 4 x 2 cm, sterling silver, 14-karat red gold washer,
copper, fine silver; etched, bezel set
Photo by Robert Diamante

soldering

To adhere pin backs to brooches,
I use a low temperature paste solder
that comes in a tube. The tube solder
is easy to apply to the surface of clean
metal. Squeeze out a small length of
paste, and position a nickel or sterling
silver pin back on the solder. From a
distance, heat the area to be soldered
either from the top or the bottom.
The solder will start to flow very fast
once you see it becoming a shiny liquid.
At this point, the solder is molten and
the connection should be secure. Wait
for the solder to cool and then clean
the area.

forging metals

To forge metal is to move and shape it
with a hammer. You can anneal metal
prior to forging it or not. Try both
methods and determine what works
best for you.

In some of the projects I've designed,
you'll forge the rough edges of cut
sheet metal to create a smooth deckled
effect. Pulling the hammer across the
edge as you strike it creates a thinner,
more fluid contour. Keep in mind that
forging work hardens metal, and you
may need to anneal a piece during the
forging process.

Wire can be forged or hammered flat.
Hammer cut wire ends flat to create
paddles, or hammer the balled wire
ends to create flat circles.

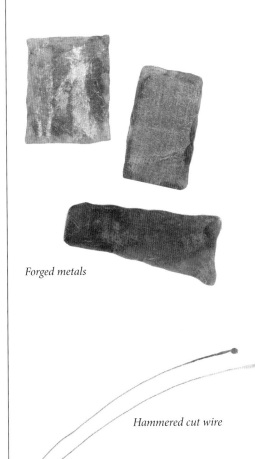

Forged metals

Hammered cut wire

Form wire into a shape of your choice, and then hammer the wire to secure the shape. Once the forged wire is work hardened, the wire is no longer pliable. This is a great method for creating wire swirls and other unique designs. However, take care not to over-forge wire. It will weaken and become brittle if hammered too thin.

texturing metals

Textured surfaces can make a piece of handmade jewelry truly terrific. There are many tools you can use to imprint patterns and motifs into metal sheet or clay. Commercial chasing tools are manufactured with various patterns and designs—even the alphabet—or you can easily create your own. Strike the end of a chasing tool with a hammer to texture the surface of sheet or wire. Metal clay should be textured before it is dried and fired. The gauge, type, and condition of the metal all play a role in how a texture is formed. Once you determine how the tools, the material, and your skill level interact, you can let your creative juices flow.

rolling mill

The rolling mill is a great device for texturing sheet metal. Use it to transfer the surface design of materials such as fabric, paper towels, lace, wire, and leaves onto metal sheet. Hold the metal and the texture sheet together and set the wheels on the mill to accommodate this thickness. Turn the handle and roll the metal through the rollers, making sure you are not forcing it. A rolling mill can also be used to make sheet metal thinner. Simply roll the sheet though the mill multiple times, each time using a thinner wheel setting.

Textured metal

tip

I often wrap the "sandwich" of sheet metal and texture sheet in paper towels before rolling it through the mill. This protects the roller surface from being scratched by the metal or texture sheet.

Rolling mill

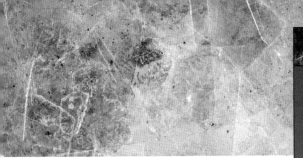

cutting sheet metal

The Tools section (page 27) showed you several different options for cutting metal. I use manual, scissor-like cutters for almost every metal (photo 1). These shears work well on material that is 24-gauge or thinner. The jeweler's saw is a more precise tool for cutting specific patterns in metal and fine details. To cut round forms or holes, I use a disk cutter (photo 2). To cut straight lines on the interior of a metal sheet, I use a sharpened flathead screwdriver (photo 3).

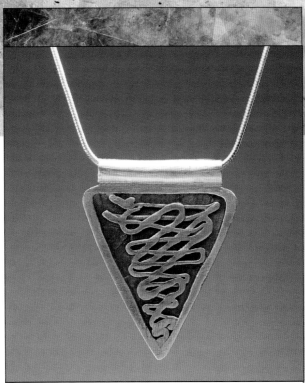

Donna Lewis *Swiggle* 2007
3.5 x 2.5 x 1.5 cm, silver clay, 24-karat gold, patina;
textured, constructed, layered, fired, kum boo
Photo by artist

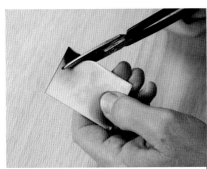

1

3

2

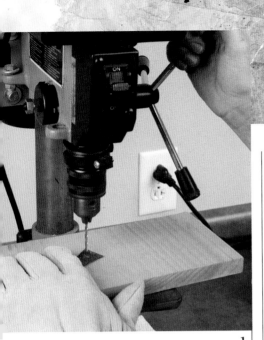

1

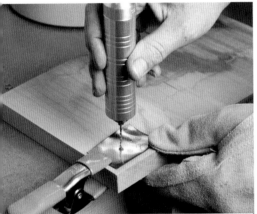

2

3

piercing sheet metal

Drilling holes into most types of metals is easy. In most instances, you'll need to clamp or hold the sheet metal piece on top of a wood block. The block provides a place for the bit to go once it breaks through the metal. Always wear safety gloves and eye protection when drilling metal. I often use a drill press (photo 1), which is a stationary tool comprised of a mounted drill and a handle. Moving the handle controls the action of the drill bit. A drill press lets you create holes with accuracy and precision and works on both sheet and clay. You can also use a high-speed, flexible shaft machine to drill holes in metal sheet and clay (photo 2). Manual ways to create holes in metal sheet include using a punch (photo 3), an awl, or a disk cutter.

WORKING WITH METAL CLAY

The three types of metal clay—bronze, copper, and silver—are very similar in their abilities. All can be used with other metals and all work well in slab construction, hollow forming, and texturing. The biggest differences between the clays, other than appearance, are their firing schedules and methods and their consistencies. The use of metal clay with sheet metal and wire is limited only by the metal's melting point.

metal clay consistency

Silver clay dries out much faster than bronze or copper clay. Because of this, silver clay needs to be kept in an airtight container when not in use. Artists will often place a slightly moist object, such as a damp sponge or paper towel, in the container with the metal clay to keep it hydrated. The clay should not get too wet, however, as it will break down and become sticky. If metal clay becomes too dry to work with, you can regenerate it by slowly mixing in some water.

In basic applications, bronze and copper clay are moist enough to stick together without the use of slip (thin clay "glue"). The drawback to this extra moisture is that bronze and copper clays are more likely to stick to work surfaces, tools, and your fingers. No matter what clay you use, always rub a light coating of lubricant over every surface the clay will touch.

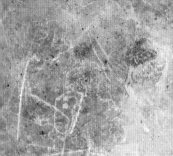

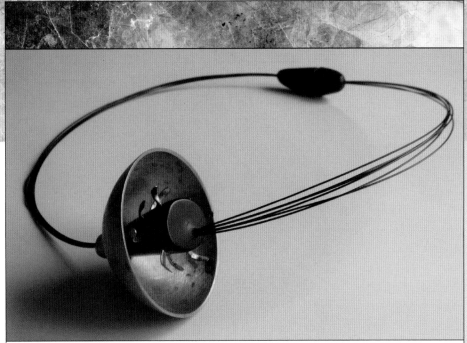

rolling slabs

You use the same method to roll slabs for all three types of metal clay. Photo 4 shows silver clay before it is rolled out to a three-playing-card thickness. I like to use plastic slats that are equivalent to the thickness of three playing cards. The plastic slats give you more rolling space and do not slip as you roll the clay.

4

step by step

1 Place a sheet of copper on your worktable. (This rigid surface will allow you to transport the wet clay to a drying area without disturbing it.) Place a nonstick surface over the copper sheet. Lightly coat the nonstick surface and the roller with lubricant. Slide it under the work surface before you begin.

2 Place two stacks of playing cards, each three-cards thick, on the nonstick surface. All of the projects in this book use the same three-card thickness. Use white slats if you prefer (photo 5).

3 Separate the lump of metal clay into a manageable amount. Store the clay you are not using in an airtight container. Place the lump of clay between the two stacks of cards.

4 Gently press the lump with the roller and begin to roll it flat. Roll the clay in one direction, and then carefully pull the clay off the surface. Reposition it in the opposite direction, and roll it flat. The card or slat stacks ensure that the rolled clay has a consistent thickness.

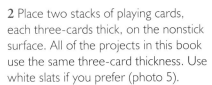

5

Imprinted clay

Christine H. Mackellar *Blossom Pendant* 2009
6.4 x 5.1 x 1.3 cm, sterling silver, 18-karat gold, 22-karat gold,
quartz; roller printed, fabricated
Photo by Hap Sakwa

Stamping

applying texture

Once you've rolled a flat slab of clay, the possibilities are endless. Add texture, cut shapes, build forms, and much, much more. Everyday items, such as ballpoint pens, coins, shells, keys, and rubber stamps can be used to imprint textures and designs in metal clay. Lubricate the surface of whatever tool you use so it won't stick to the clay.

Most often, I texture the clay before cutting the final shapes. This way, the cut remains precise and isn't altered by texturing. Sometimes I want uneven edges. In this case, I cut out the shapes first, and then add texture. Try both ways to see what you prefer.

imprinting

Use your hands to lightly press the desired item into the rolled metal clay slab, or use a roller with consistent pressure to gently roll over the item and imprint its texture.

stamping

Completely cover the surface of the stamp with a light coat of lubricant, and then press it into the clay slab. If you want to make your own unique rubber stamps, use a cutter to carve soft linoleum.

texture plates

Brass texture plates are commercially manufactured for use in rolling mills to transfer textures onto sheet metal. They are inexpensive, come in a wide range of patterns, and are sold through jewelry suppliers. These plates also work beautifully to texture metal clay slabs. Gently press the plates into the clay with your hands or with a roller.

Texture plates

cutting metal clay

Wet or moist clay is beautifully easy to cut, freeing you to create any shape imaginable. When cutting clay with a craft knife, it's best to work on top of a self-healing cutting surface. If cutting on other nonstick surfaces, be sure not to put too much pressure on the craft knife or you will cut through the mat.

freehand

Cut out any shape desired freehand using a craft knife, awl, or any sharp edge. The cutting instrument needs to be lubricated first so it will slide through the clay with ease.

stencils & templates

Using a stencil, template, or any traceable item can be helpful for cutting precise shapes.

I often cut out a stencil from paper or cardboard when constructing several similar pieces, such as for the Copper Vessel Pendant on page 115, or to ensure that I cut a very specific shape, such as in Figure Study on page 121. Make sure a stencil is cut and ready before you unwrap the clay, so it will not be left out too long and become dry.

tearing

Because of my background in fiber, I love free flowing edges. Tearing metal clay creates a wonderful unfussy edge. Lay a clay slab over an object, such as a rubber stamp, and pull the excess clay away from the edge. This method is used in Relic Pendant on page 112, which features tear-away copper clay with silver sheet metal.

Using stencils

Freehand

Tearing

Pierced metal clay

Metal clay beads

piercing metal clay

There are a variety of ways to pierce holes in metal clay. You can create holes while the clay is wet, when the clay is dry, and even after the clay is fired.

straws & tubing

Using a plastic straw or tube is the simplest way to make a hole in metal clay. Once you form a slab, pierce the wet clay with a straw in the same manner you would use a cookie cutter (photo 1). If the clay sticks in the straw's hole, try collapsing the straw as you press out the clay.

drilling unfired clay

This method is my least favorite, probably because I have a heavy hand, but it makes a beautiful hole. Place the pointed tip of a drill bit on the surface of the dry clay and gently roll the bit between your fingers (photo 2). Work carefully so you don't break the unfired clay.

drilling fired clay

You can use a high-speed drill or drill press to make holes in fired metal clay (photo 3), but I recommend making holes, or at least poking a pilot hole, before firing if at all possible. Thick bronze and copper clay pieces are difficult to drill with small, jeweler's size drill bits.

shaping metal clay

Because of its malleability, metal clay can be easily sculpted into dimensional forms, both solid and hollow. Fabricating the same forms with sheet metal would be much more difficult. Bronze, copper, and silver clay can be connected and sculpted.

1

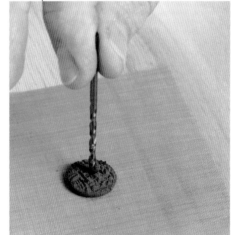

2

3

Todd Pownell Untitled 2008
1.4 x 2.2 x 2.3 cm, sterling silver, 24-karat yellow gold,
white and black diamonds
Photo by artist

metal clay slip

Slip is a watered down version of metal clay with a sticky consistency that is used to adhere seams, make repairs, and secure connections. Silver clay slip is available commercially in a jar or syringe. You can easily make your own slip out of any of the three metal clays by adding distilled or purified water to a small amount of clay. The consistency should be pasty. Store your slip in an airtight container so you can reuse it and add more as needed. Always store your slips in separate containers. The different metal clays should not be mixed together.

Gently apply commercial silver slip or slip made from clay or powder and water to the areas you need to connect, using a soft bristle paintbrush. Once the connection is made, smooth the area with the brush and let the clay dry. Follow the same process to apply slip with a syringe.

making metal clay beads

There are many ways to make metal clay beads. Use them to put your personal touch on every project.

flat beads

Flat, doughnut-style beads are the easiest type to make, and you can form them out of any metal clay. The directions below use two sizes of drinking straws, but you can use stencils, circle templates, or disk cutters to make beads with larger diameters.

step by step

1 Roll out a small slab of metal clay.

2 Use a plastic straw with a large diameter to cut out a clay disk.

3 Position a plastic straw with a small diameter in the center of the clay disk and press the small straw down to create a hole.

Using metal clay slip

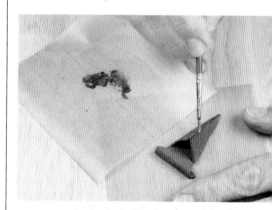

Shaping flat beads

rolled beads

Rolled beads can be made from any type of metal clay. Copper and bronze clays are the easiest to use because no slip is required. With silver clay, a little slip is needed to hold the roll together. Rolled beads can be used to embellish a piece of jewelry or as the featured element, as seen in Draped Copper Trio on page 118.

Rolled beads

step by step

1 Roll a slab of metal clay. Add texture to the slab if desired.

2 Using a sharp craft knife, cut random triangular shapes or rectangles that decrease in width from the metal clay slab. These shapes should be just long enough to encircle a drinking straw one and one-half times.

3 Starting with the wider end of one cut shape, gently roll the metal clay around a straw until the piece is secure. If using silver clay, paint a bit of slip on the bead as you roll it. Leave the wrapped bead on the straw to dry.

4 Roll additional metal clay shapes into beads on the same straw. Once all beads are dry, remove them from the straw before firing the clay.

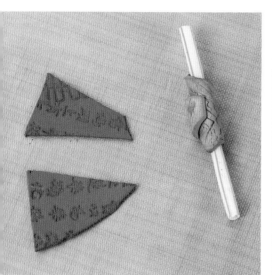

Rolling metal clay beads

Pressed charm beads

pressed charm beads

This method produces beads with nice rounded and rolled edges with organic contours. The Confetti Bracelet on page 96 shows the variety of styles and sizes you can achieve with charm beads.

step by step

1 Divide the metal clay of your choice into small amounts.

2 One at a time, roll the small amounts of metal clay in your fingers to form individual balls.

3 Use your finger or thumb to press each ball flat. Add texture to flattened metal clay if desired.

4 Either use an awl to poke a pilot hole in each bead or use a small straw to create a finished hole.

Lori Meg Gottlieb *Curly Bark Bracelet* 2009
2 x 7.5 x 0.25 cm, sterling silver, 22-karat bimetal; hammered, forged, fabricated
Photo by Hap Sakwa

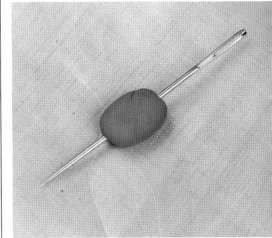

Lump bead

lump beads

These beads are used as a larger focal bead as seen in Copper Ring on page 123, or as accents in jewelry pieces.

step by step

1 Form a lump of metal clay into a ball or a rectangle.

2 Poke a bamboo skewer or a small straw through the metal clay ball or rectangle to create the hole for the bead.

3 Sculpt the clay bead to the desired length, thickness, and shape. Texture the clay if desired. Let the bead dry on the straw.

4 Remove the dry bead from the straw before firing.

metal clay sheet

Metal clay sheet is a flexible paper-like material that does not dry out as fast as lump clay. Currently, it is only available in silver. This material is a great addition to my work as it is well suited for weaving and other textile-related techniques.

Woven metal clay sheet

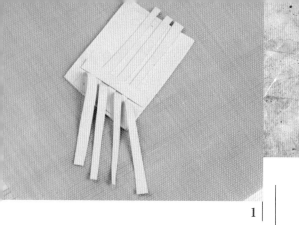

1

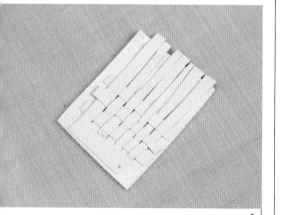

2

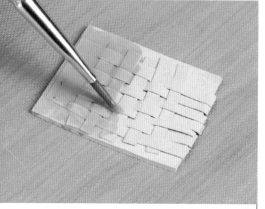

3

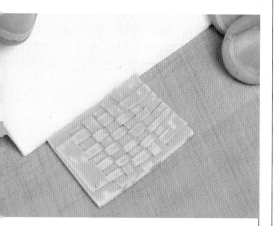

4

weaving metal clay sheet

When weaving with metal clay sheet, cut spokes (fringe) into the paper clay, stopping short of cutting all the way through to create a solid end. Secure the solid end to a clay body with a small amount of water. Next, thread dry weavers through the fringe until an entire grid is woven (photos 1 and 2).

Gently lifting the cut spokes, keep threading the paper strips or wire weavers through the spokes.

Secure the grid by gently dabbing its surface with a wet paintbrush (photo 3).

Finish by gently placing a paper towel on the side of the woven grid to wick the water away from the surface and ensure a good connection.

You can cut other shapes and designs from the sheet clay and apply them to the surface of any wet clay body with a small amount of water. Once the sheet clay is attached, avoid putting any pressure on it. It is extremely fragile until it dries (photo 4).

drying metal clay

Metal clay must be dry before it can be fired. There are many ways to dry your pieces.

air drying

It can take a while for metal clay to fully air dry, but it is a good method to use if a piece has a lot of connections. You don't want to dry a complex piece too fast and run the risk of having it crack.

forced air drying

Forced air-drying methods speed up the process by employing devices that add heat or air or both. Food dehydrators, coffee mug warmers, hair dryers, or fans are all commonly used devices. Always operate these devices with caution and do not let them get too hot. Also, handle dried pieces with care, as they are often hot to the touch.

In my work, I place metal clay pieces in a cardboard container that has a hole cut in its lid. I insert the nozzle of a hair dryer through this hole and dry my pieces. I have found it extremely helpful to place wet metal clay pieces on top of a sheet of copper to dry. As the sheet metal is heated, it radiates heat which helps dry the clay. Metal clay that isn't completely dry will leave a sweat mark on the copper sheet. Monitoring the presence of a sweat mark is an easy way to check if a piece of metal clay is completely dry before placing it in the kiln.

Rebecca A. McLaughlin Neigher *Boutonniere* 2008
5 x 5 x 1.3 cm, nickel silver, red brass, sterling silver, freshwater pearl;
fabricated, textured, forged, soldered
Photo by artist

working dry & making connections

For some projects, such as the Lattice Bead Bracelet on page 92 and Copper Vessel Pendant on page 115, individual metal clay elements need to be dried before they are assembled into the final piece of jewelry. You may need to sand the surface of the elements before connecting them with slip.

To sand the edges of dried metal clay, place a piece of sandpaper face up on a hard work surface. Gently hold the piece in your hand and refine its edges on the sandpaper (photo 5). The metal clay dust and particles produced from sanding makes great slip so save all the dust for this purpose.

firing metal clay

Follow the recommended firing schedules for the individual types of metal clay. Keep in mind that all clay must be completely dry before it is fired. Silver clay pieces are fired individually in the kiln or in groups, using kiln furniture. Bronze and copper clays are imbedded in activated carbon inside a stainless steel container (photo 6) and then fired.

Use coconut-based carbon for the copper clay and either coconut- or coal-based carbon for the bronze. When placing pieces in the carbon, make sure to leave about 1 inch (2.5 cm) of space between them and between multiple layers. Fill the entire container with carbon and make sure the lid fits properly.

finishing metal sheet & metal clay

Brass brushes, files, burnishers, and grinders are just a few of the tools used to finish the surface of sheet metal and fired metal clay. When using a bench grinder, make sure to hold the piece at a 45° angle, going with the rotation of the wheel. Always use the plastic guard and secure clothing and hair away from the wheel. Ring clamps can be useful for holding small metal pieces to avoid finger burns (photo 7). When using the bench grinder, always wear a dust mask and eye protection, keep your fingers away from the wheel, and keep the area clear of clutter.

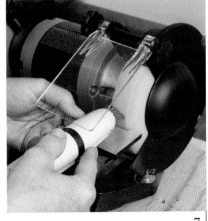

So Young Park *Oriental Bloom Series* 2008
5 x 7 x 3 cm, 24-karat gold leaf, sterling silver, 18-karat yellow gold
Photo by artist

When fired and removed from the kiln, silver clay has a matte white finish, whereas bronze and copper clays display a wide spectrum of colors. Silver clay needs to be polished to smooth and refine its porous texture. The other clays can be left with their fired patina. Often, I partially polish my bronze and clay pieces for contrast.

My favorite tool is a bench grinder with a de-burring wheel attachment. It shines and cleans all types of metal better than any other tool I have found. Make sure to clean the back of all metal pieces with a brass brush or cleaner so firescale, patinas, and/or heat treatments won't rub off onto skin or clothing.

APPLYING PATINAS

A patina is any fading, darkening, or other signs of age that appear on metal. The chemical process by which a patina forms is called patination, and a work of art that bares a patina is patinated. Patinas are commonly the result of a chemical compound forming on a metal surface. In nature, this process occurs over time due to exposure to the elements, but manmade patinas can also be deliberately applied. Some patinas are temporary and can change or flake off the surface. Others actually change the metal and are permanent. Partially buffing off a patina allows the natural metal to show through, creating more detail and depth on the surface.

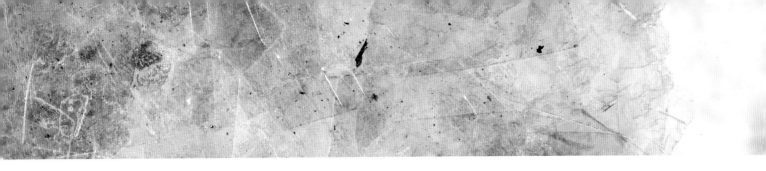

tips

Patinas are achieved faster and more successfully if the metal has been work-hardened, textured, or heated prior to application. If metal is new, smooth, and has not been worked or heated, it has a tendency to resist the patina and/or the process will take longer.

Complete all of your metalwork before applying a patina. Otherwise, the patina will be disturbed or altered.

Chains, jump rings, wires, and findings can also be patinated.

Silver will "tarnish" over time, a natural oxidizing process that darkens and dulls the metal.

green patina

The common green patina found on copper is the result of a slow chemical process that produces a basic carbonate. It's a result of weather, elements, and water exposure. You can apply a green patina solution to speed up the process and achieve similar coloration. Chlorides are the active ingredients in these commercial patinas. Using a matte fixative helps to adhere the green patina to the metal and inhibit flaking. Greens, yellows, browns, and oranges will form on pure copper objects, as well as alloys that contain copper, such as bronze or brass. When green patina solution is applied to silver, a light yellow-gold color is achieved.

bronze & copper clay patinas

When fired, bronze and copper clay are beautifully colored. Patinas develop both when the hot pieces are quenched in cold water and when the pieces are left to completely cool in the firing container. (If you choose to quench hot clay pieces in order to create a patina, be sure to take all safety precautions.)

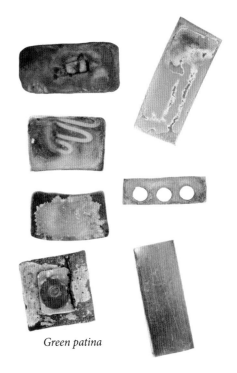

Green patina

Bronze & copper clay patinas

Liver of sulfur patinas

Emily B. Miller Untitled 2008
2.6 x 2.4 x 0.5 cm, fine silver, 23.5-karat gold, copper
spacers, brass nuts and bolts, sterling silver
Photo by Edward Miller

liver of sulfur patina

Jewelers frequently use sulfur compounds to emphasize textures and enhance details. It's an exceptionally nice solution to work with and makes a variety of patina hues possible. Liver of sulfur will change the color of silver and copper sheet and clay. Immersing the metal in the solution for a prolonged time produces deep, rich browns and blacks. Shorter, well-monitored immersions can lead to brilliant purples, reds, and yellows.

You can purchase liver of sulfur as a ready-to-use liquid or you can simply mix the solid form with water. I prefer making my own solution, mixing as much as needed at any given time. Many factors effect how metal reacts to this patina, including how much it has been worked, its gauge, and its texture.

step by step

Before you begin: Liver of sulfur solution emits an unpleasant odor, similar to rotten eggs, so be certain to work in a well-ventilated area.

1 Carefully pour hot or boiling water into a heat-resistant container.

2 Add a small chunk of liver of sulfur to the hot water and let it dissolve.

3 Option I: Pick up the metal (sheet or fired clay) with tongs and dip it into the liver of sulfur solution. Quickly move the metal in and out of the solution and watch the patina gradually form until you are satisfied with the result.

Option 2: Apply the solution with a soft bristle paintbrush and monitor the development of the coloration (photo 1).

4 Rinse the metal in water after the desired patina is achieved.

1

commercial black patina

The active agent in commercial blackening solution is hydrochloric acid. You can apply this solution to silver, copper, or bronze sheet or fired clay. Contact with the solution will immediately cause the metals to blacken (much quicker than liver of sulfur). Textures in the metal can be highlighted through buffing, polishing, cleaning, tumbling, and burnishing. Keep in mind that hydrochloric acid is far more dangerous than the liver of sulfur, so carefully read and follow the manufacturer's instructions.

heated patinas

Unheated and untextured metal will not be receptive to deep heat and chemical patinas. If you anneal and texture the metal and then apply the patina, its effect can be deliberately accelerated. Heating the metal multiple times will bring out more vibrant colors. If you use a propane torch to activate a patina solution, do so outside or in a well-ventilated area with an exhaust fan to cut down on fumes. Use old pliers to hold the metal, and move it in and out of the torch flame. Depending on the patina used, the heat-induced colors will range from greens, yellows, and oranges to deep blues, reds, and purples. By reheating fired clay pieces, interesting and intense color variations can be produced.

Years ago I accidentally discovered a very nontraditional patina. Dry cat food was spilled on a piece of copper foil that I was about to patina with a torch. Instead of pushing the cat food off the surface, I torched the foil with the cat food on it. (The oil in the cat food kept it from moving.) Soldering heat radiated around the kibble and created amazing colors. Try it. It's fun!

Commercial black patina

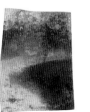

Heated patina

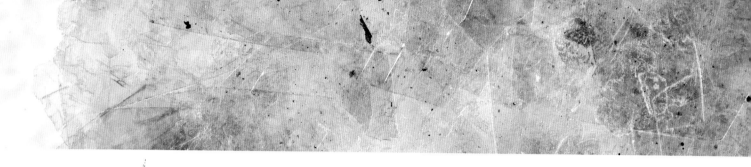

figure a

figure b

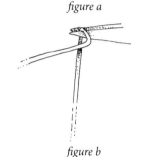

figure c

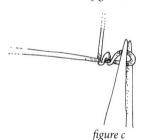

figure d

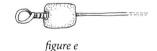

figure e

figure f

WORKING WITH WIRE

Wire is a great addition to contemporary mixed metal jewelry. I love wire because I feel at home with stitching. Wire allows me to incorporate many of the basketry and fiber techniques that I am familiar with. Wire also gives detail to jewelry and allows you to make many creative connections.

wrapping a wire loop

I frequently wrap wire loops in the shape of a teardrop. This is not the traditional method, but suits my style very well.

step by step

1 Hold the wire with needle- or chain-nose pliers where you want to create the loop (figure A).

2 Pull one end of the wire around one tip of the pliers, making a loop the size you desire and ending at a 90° angle to the other wire end (figure B).

3 Reposition the pliers to hold the loop (figure C).

4 Secure the end of the wire that made the loop by wrapping it tightly and consistently away from the loop, along the wire (figure D).

5 Cut the wire end close to the wrap with flush wire cutters.

6 Using pliers, tightly crimp the wrapped wire to remove any sharp ends (figure E).

7 If desired, add beads between wrapped loops or onto the wire before making a wrapped loop (figure F).

tips & variations

Change the sizes and shapes of the wrapped loops to achieve a variety of styles. When adding beads on a wire, leave enough extra wire to make a wrapped loop.

Connect wrapped loops to each other for an attractive design.

Use wrapped loops to hold a neck chain.

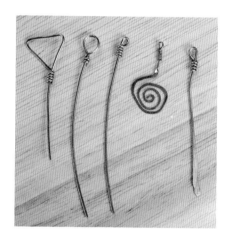

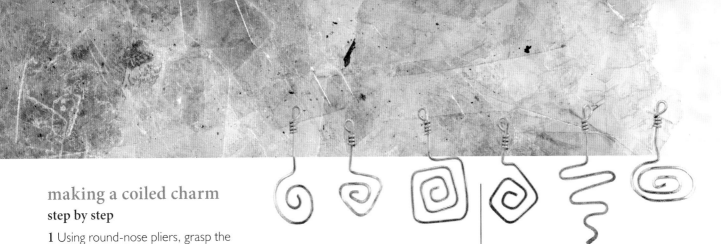

making a coiled charm
step by step

1 Using round-nose pliers, grasp the end of a 5-inch (12.7 cm) piece of wire. Use pliers or your fingers to pull the opposite end of the wire around to form a small circle. This is the base of a flat coil (figure G).

2 Continue to wrap the wire in a circle, increasing the size of the coil and leaving space between the wires with each rotation (figure H).

3 Once the coil reaches the desired size, bend the wire at a 90° angle. Make a wrapped loop at the end of the wire to create a charm (figures I and J).

4 Hammer gently, forging the charm to harden the wire. If you use the ball part of the ball-peen hammer you can achieve a nice texture for the charm.

You can create charms of many shapes with wire.

wrapping beads on head pins

Thread beads onto headpins or wires with paddled or balled ends. Make a simple wire wrap, and use these components to embellish your jewelry.

opening jump rings & ear wires

Use two pairs of pliers to grasp the wire ring on either side of the split. Twist the wire ends open rather than pulling them apart. This method maintains the shape of the ring and the strength of the metal.

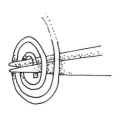

figure g

figure h

figure i

figure j

mixing sheet metal

The first five step-by-step projects in this book are all designed with sheet metal to give you the opportunity to use and practice basic metalworking techniques. The following projects add metal clay to the mix, but for now, it's all about cutting, shaping, wrapping, and folding sheet. (Pssst: No soldering is required!)

If you're a true beginner, I recommend closely following the instructions to understand the techniques and sharpen your skills. With experience, it will be very easy for you to expand on the concepts and design unique jewelry that reflects your style. If you've worked with metal before, you may want to explore variations, substitutions, or more complex embellishments.

The project Disk Earrings explores basic cutout shapes. You'll learn to assemble layers of disks in a variety of styles, and you'll have the opportunity to make your own ear wires. Due to its endless creative potential, this simple project may become one of your favorites.

The Trellis Pendant begins as a flat organic shape and is bent into an interesting three-dimensional object. Horizontal wires across the piece create a ladder effect and offer a valuable lesson in balling wire ends.

In the Currency Pendant, a planned mistake becomes a wonderful design detail. An intentional tear in the metal is repaired with small eyelets to give the project an industrial edge. You'll capture found objects between metal pieces, secure them with nuts and bolts, and in the process, explore cold connections.

A series of wire connections and wrapped loops makes Orbit Bracelet appear more complicated than it actually is. This is your chance to master the disk cutter and dapping block, handy skills to use in your own custom designs.

The Catch & Keep Pendant is one of my favorites because it draws on my first love: weaving. A simple silver fold showcases found objects, while a carefully stitched edge gives the piece a signature style.

Several project variations feature metal clay as an alternate material or decorative element. Once you're comfortable with metal clay, revisit these projects and imagine how they can be adapted. You'll soon appreciate how to enhance each design with your own style and skills.

disk earrings

techniques

Annealing
Heat patina
Cutting
Forging
Dapping
Drilling
Wirework

materials

Copper sheet, 24 gauge
Brass sheet, 26 gauge
Silver sheet, 30 gauge

Half-hard sterling silver
wire, 20 gauge, 12 inches
(30.5 cm) for one pair
of each style

Spacer beads (optional)

tools

Sheet metal kit, page 41

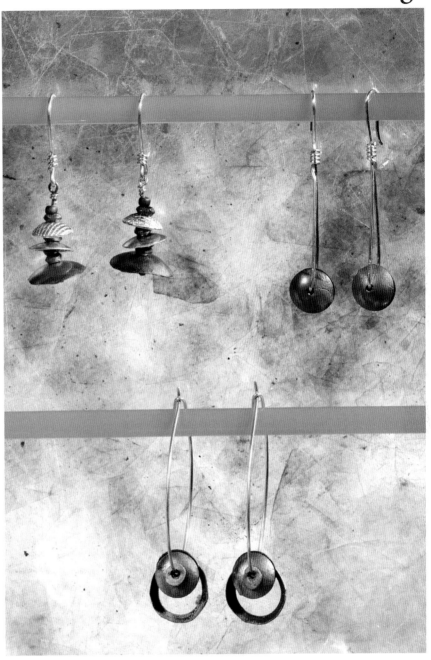

You'll be amazed at how many beautiful earrings you can make
by combining a variety of sheet metal shapes with half-hard silver
ear wires. Use a disk cutter and dapping block to explore the design
possibilities of the round shape, or achieve a variety of other forms
with metal sheet cutters.

disk earrings

step by step

making the metal disks

1 Put on your safety glasses and leather gloves, and pick up one copper sheet with the old pliers. Anneal the copper with the propane torch. Flash the sheet with the torch flame to patina the copper surface. Move the piece in and out of the flame to heat and soften it and also create color, then quench it in water. (Brass and silver sheets do not need to be treated.)

2 Use metal snips to cut the copper, brass, and silver sheets into several small pieces. With the hammer and disk cutter, punch out a collection of various sized disks from the small metal pieces (photo 1).

3 If desired, hammer the disks to give them texture and to forge their edges (photo 2). You can create a deckled effect or smooth textures. Rough edges can be re-cut or filed smooth, then hammered again.

4 Punch or drill a $1/16$-inch (1.6 mm) hole in each disk. Center the hole or locate it wherever you would like the pieces to hang.

5 One at a time, place the metal disks in the dapping block. Hammer the end of the corresponding dapping tool to create a domed shape (photo 3). If your hole becomes distorted from hammering, drill it with a $1/16$-inch (1.6 mm) bit, or bore it out with an awl.

making round-hoop earrings

1 Cut two lengths of sterling silver wire, each approximately $1 1/2$ inches (3.8 cm) long. Use the bench grinder to smooth all four ends of the two wires.

2 Using needle-nose or round-nose pliers, bend the ends of each wire around to meet each other in a circle.

3 Slide the metal disks onto the hoops with the small pieces at the front of the earrings. If desired, add spacer beads between the metal disks to give the earrings more dimension (figure A). Repeat this process with the second wire. Gently hammer both wire hoops to harden them.

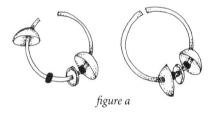

figure a

1

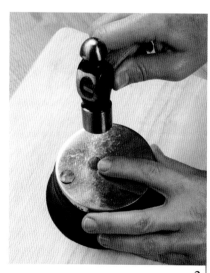

2

3

4 Use needle-nose pliers to create a hook at one end of each hoop (figure B). Make a hook in the opposite end of each hoop (figure C) and feed it through the loop to close the earrings.

figure b   *figure c*

making vertically stacked earrings

1 Cut 3 to 4 inches (7.6 to 10.2 cm) of silver wire, and burn a ball on one end. Stack several disks with spacer beads between each one for dimension; the ball at the end of the wire will hold them in place (figure D). Complete the top with a wrapped loop (figure E). Finish the earrings by adding commercial or handmade French-hook ear wires.

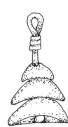

figure d   *figure e*

making horizontal earrings

1 Cut 4 inches (10.2 cm) of silver wire. Bend the wire 1 to 1½ inches (2.5 to 3.8 cm) from one end at a 90° angle. Thread the disks, and bend the other side of the wire at a 90° angle close to the disks, but not too tight, to allow movement (figure F). Wrap the shorter of the two wires around the longer one, and cut (figure G). Finish the last wire with a wrapped loop (figure H). Attach ear wires.

figure f

figure g

figure h

variations

Use alternate shapes, metals, and accent beads for endless design possibilities. Create and stamp bronze-, copper-, or silver-clay disks to make your own unique pieces.

trellis pendant

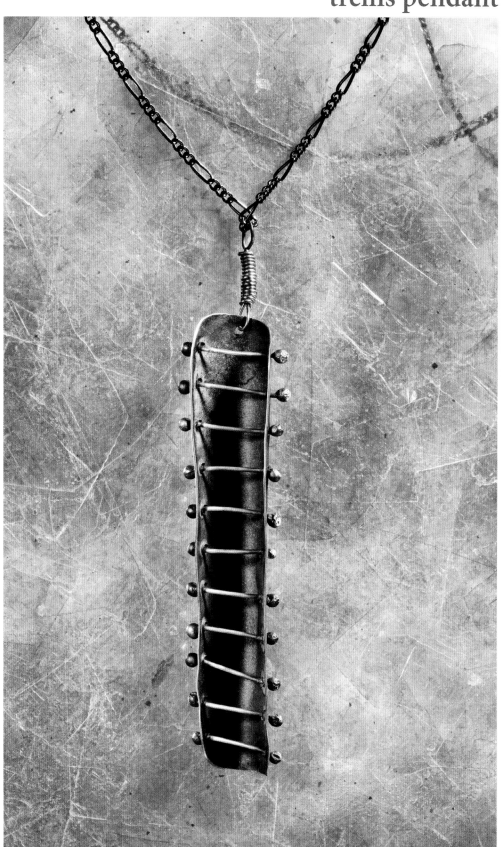

Create simple, whimsical shapes with copper sheets and wire. Once assembled, bend and manipulate the form to alter its shape for multiple styles. For more variation, display the necklace facing in or out, and hang it horizontally or vertically.

step by step

1 Prepare the copper sheet by cutting it with metal snips into an organic shape, as seen in figure A, approximately 1 to 1½ x 2½ to 3 inches (2.5 to 3.8 x 6.4 to 7.6 cm).

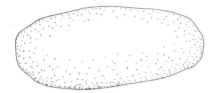

figure a

2 Pick up the copper piece with the old pliers. Flash the flame of the propane torch onto the surface of the copper to create a heat patina. Move the copper piece in and out of the flame to create color. Quench the piece in cold water.

3 Use the hammer and steel block or anvil to forge the edges of the copper piece, creating a deckled effect (photo 1). Use the metal file to smooth the edges. Cut away any sharp edges with the metal snips. Continue forging the piece until it is smooth.

4 Reheat the copper to make it soft and easier to bend. Use the hole punch to puncture a parallel, evenly spaced row of holes on each side of the piece, approximately ⅛ inch (3 mm) from the edge. These will later hold the pendant's horizontal wires. (You can also drill the holes, but I find the punch method easier.) Punch one small hole at the top of the piece for the bail.

5 Bend the long, punched sides of the copper sheet into a gentle curve with pliers (photo 2), leaving about a ½-inch (1.3 cm) gap.

6 Count the holes along one side, and cut that many pieces of 20- or 18-gauge wire, each approximately 2 to 3 inches (5.1 to 7.6 cm) long. Use the propane torch to ball one end of each wire. As shown in figure B, thread the wires through the holes on one side of the piece and out the other parallel hole.

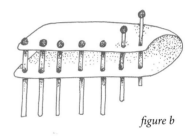

figure b

1

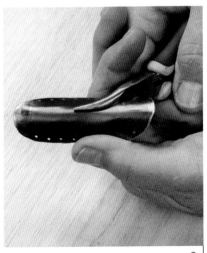

2

trellis pendant

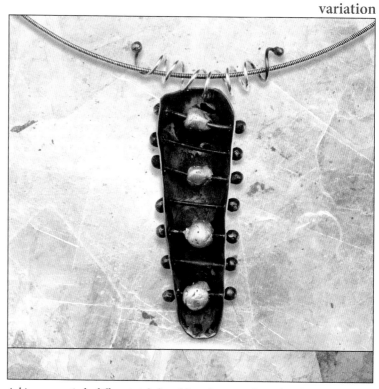

7 Cut the unballed ends of the wire about ½ inch (1.3 cm) from where they exit the holes. Hold the piece with the old pliers and ball the opposite ends of wire (photo 3). Start at the far end, and work towards the wire closest to you. Have patience and don't worry about the amount of heat you apply to the metal. It will turn black.

8 When all the balls have been created, put the piece back into the flame to create color. Gently place it in and out of the fire, as shown in photo 4, and then quench it in cold water.

9 Attach a jump ring or bail of your choice and then string the pendant on a cord or chain. The sample project features a wire-wrapped bail using mixed metals.

Achieve an entirely different style by adding clay or sterling silver beads to the wires. Here's how: Make small balls of clay by kneading them into little circles. After threading the wires through one side of the piece (step 6), secure the clay balls on the desired wires. Thread the wires through the holes on the other side of the piece. Allow the clay balls to dry completely before firing the piece in a kiln or with a torch.

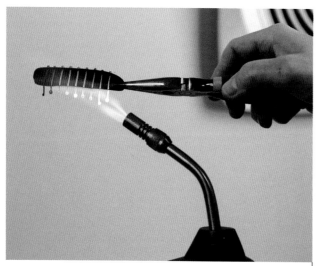

3

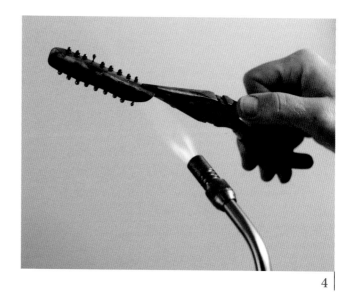

4

currency pendant

Capture your favorite found coin inside copper sheets, and you've got a simple necklace with an eye-catching design. Achieve the rustic quality by tearing and repairing the piece. Not only a design element, this technique also works well for structural repairs, and can be used to patch metal clay.

currency pendant

techniques

Annealing
Heat patina
Cutting
Texturing
Drilling or punching
Setting eyelets
Cold connecting

materials

Copper sheet,
24 gauge, 2 pieces,
each approximately
2½ to 3 inches
(6.4 to 7.6 cm) square

Coin

Silver or brass sheet,
24 gauge, 2 small pieces,
each approximately
½ inch (1.3 cm) square

4 miniature eyelets

5 nut and bolt sets,
⅛ inch (3 mm)

Chain or cord
of your choice

tools

Sheet metal kit, page 41

Jeweler's saw and
saw blades

Flathead screwdriver
(optional)

step by step

1 Anneal and heat-treat the copper sheets with the propane torch.

2 Measure the diameter of your coin. Use the disk cutter to cut two circles from the copper sheets, each approximately ⅛ inch to ¼ inch (3 to 6 mm) smaller than the diameter of the coin. These will be the inner circles of the piece, or the window. Now use metal snips to cut around the outside of these circles. This time, cut approximately ¼ to ½ inch (6 mm to 1.3 cm) larger than your coin. Allow enough room in your frame to accommodate bolts used to assemble the necklace later (photo 1).

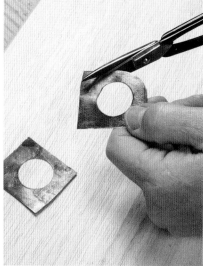

1

3 Create texture on the surfaces of the round copper frames with the hammer and steel block or anvil as seen in figure A. File the edges smooth. Use the scissors to create a tear or break in each circle.

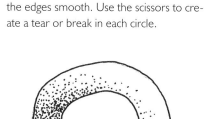

figure a

4 Cut two small rectangular pieces of silver or brass to place over the tears in the circles, as if patching a repair. File the edges smooth. Punch two holes in each of the rectangles (photo 2).

2

5 Line up the two holes on each small rectangular piece, and use them as a guide to punch holes in the two large circles as seen in figure B. Set the eyelets in these holes, and "repair" both circles.

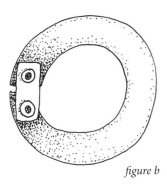

figure b

6 Decide where to place holes for the nuts and bolts, depending on the desired style and size of the piece. I created five holes around each circle to secure the coin. Drill these holes with the ⅛-inch (3 mm) drill bit or the ⅛-inch (3 mm) hole punch. Use these holes as a template, and drill matching holes in the second circle.

7 Assemble the necklace by layering the back circle, the coin, and then the top circle. Screw the nuts and bolts into the piece using your fingers or a flathead screwdriver (photo 3).

3

8 Thread the neck chain through the inside of the piece around one of the bolts.

Before you repair torn sheet metal or clay, determine how many patches you think the design will require. I sometimes find it interesting to allow a large gap to be visible through several patches, as shown in the copper and silver brooch.

orbit bracelet

techniques
Annealing
Cutting
Punching
Forging
Balling wire
Wirework

materials
Any combination
of copper, brass,
or sterling sheets,
24 gauge, 6 x 6 inches
(15.2 x 15.2 cm),
or scrap pieces

Copper wire,
18 gauge, 3 to 4 feet
(91.4 to 121.9 cm)

22 to 25 assorted
metal disk beads,
oval spacers,
or small flat beads,
each approximately
¾ inch (1.9 cm)
in diameter

tools
Sheet metal kit, page 41

You already learned the skills to design disk earrings, but this whimsical bracelet project will make you a professional disk cutter. The mix of copper, brass, and silver offers a range of stylistic options and endless creativity, all wrapped up and layered around your wrist.

step by step

1 Anneal small sections of the metal sheets. Then cut 22 to 25 small circles, approximately ½ inch (1.3 cm) in diameter each, with the disk cutters and a hammer.

2 Punch a hole in the center of each disk with the ¹/₁₆-inch (1.6 mm) hole punch. One at a time, place each metal disk in the dapping block, considering the appropriate diameter size, and dap each disk into a dome. If the holes become distorted, bore them out with an awl.

3 Cut 22 to 25 pieces of 18-gauge wire, each approximately 2½ to 3 inches (6.4 to 7.6 cm) long. Burn a ball on one end of each wire.

4 Assemble the bracelet by following the steps below:

First, thread one commercial bead and one hand-cut domed disk onto a piece of the cut wire. Pull the ball on the wire tight against the bead.

Second, place the wire on the anvil, and hammer the center area of the wire to flatten it (photo 1). This will spread the wire, create visual interest, and secure the disk in place.

Third, after flattening the middle area of the wire, make a wrapped loop on the end opposite the beads. Assemble a second disk and bead onto a new piece of wire, and insert it into the wrapped loop of the previous wire before hammering the middle section flat.

Repeat this process until you have created a chain that is approximately 20 inches (50.8 cm) long. Alternate the metal composition of the commercial beads to vary the design. I put some disks face-up and others face-down to create a variety of domes and concave shapes (figure A).

figure a

1

orbit bracelet

5 Wrap the bracelet around your wrist three times; the fit should be snug. On the last connection, attach a commercial or handmade wire hook (figures B, C, D, and photo 2).

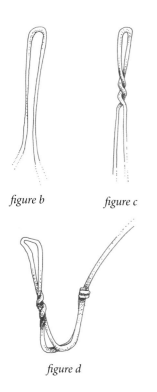

figure b   *figure c*

figure d

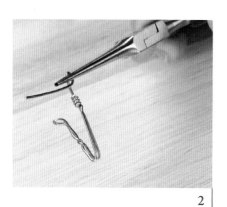

2

Achieve different styles by securing the wrapped bracelet with copper jump rings in several places, by playing with a variety of beads, or by making metal clay disks. If you'd rather leave this piece unwrapped and wear it as a necklace, that works too!

catch & keep pendant

techniques

Forging

Texturing

Using a rolling mill (optional)

Sweat soldering (optional)

Drilling or punching

Balling wire

Wirework

materials

Photocopied template

Sterling silver sheet,
26 gauge, 4 x 1 inches
(10.2 x 2.5 cm)

Copper, brass, or colored
craft wire, 26 gauge
and 18 gauge

Wood or other organic
found object

tools

Sheet metal kit, page 41

Rolling mill (optional)

feeling the urge to get closer to nature? Using sterling silver, create a simple triangle pendant filled with organic found objects. Line the edges with detailed wire stitching for added interest. Items can be trapped in a variety of ways by changing the metal rolls and folds.

step by step

1 Trace the photocopied template onto the silver sheet. Cut out the traced form with metal snips. Forge the silver sheet to create a deckled edge. To texture the sheet, make several small, randomly spaced dimples with an awl, or run it through a rolling mill (photo 1). If desired, sweat solder small copper or silver accent pieces to the surface for additional texture.

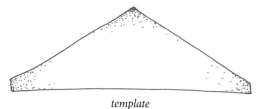

template

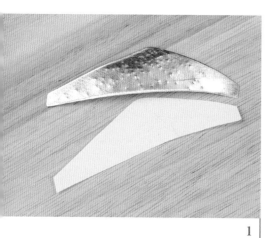

1

2 Position the sheet horizontally. With the hole punch or drill, punch holes along the tapered edge of the sheet. Start and finish about ½ to 1 inch (1.3 to 2.5 cm) from each narrow end. There should be a ¼-inch (6 mm) space between each hole, and the row of holes should be about ⅛ inch (3 mm) in from the edge of the sheet. At the widest point in the center of the silver piece, gradually bend the pendant in half using pliers.

3 Cut a piece of 18-gauge wire to extend 1 inch (2.5 cm) beyond the row of holes on each end of the metal sheet. Burn balls on both ends of the wire. This wire is your spoke.

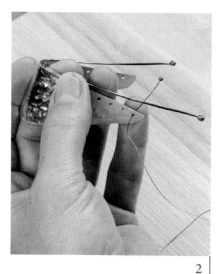

2

4 Cut a 4- to 5-foot-long (10.2 to 152.4 cm) piece of the 26-gauge wire. Burn a ball on one end of the wire. Determine which side is going to be the front of the pendant. Thread the wire through the top hole (narrow end) of the front of the pendant (photo 2).

5 Place the 18-gauge wire spoke along the edge of the pendant. Begin to secure the spoke to the pendant by wrapping the 26-gauge wire around the spoke. Feed the 26-gauge wire back through the first hole.

6 Once the spoke is secured to the edge, begin the wrap. Firmly wrap the 26-gauge wire around the spoke without allowing any space between the spoke and the metal. Continue wrapping the wire until you come to the next hole (figure A).

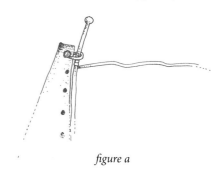

figure a

7 Stitch the wire through the second hole to secure it (figure B). Continue this process until you have wrapped and stitched through the entire row of holes on the front and back of the pendant. After threading through the last hole, secure the wire by wrapping it around several times before cutting it close to the spoke.

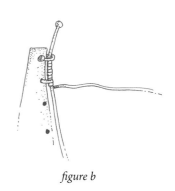

figure b

8 The ends of the 18-gauge wire can be longer than the area wrapped, as shown in this example. Simply bend the ends into a U shape for this additional detail at the top of the necklace (photo 3).

3

9 The top of the pendant can be designed in several ways. To follow the design shown here, drill or punch a hole in the center of the tapered ends about ½ inch (1.3 cm) from the top edges. Burn a ball on one end of a 12-inch (30.5 cm) piece of 26-gauge wire. Insert the wire through both holes and tightly pull the ends together. Wrap the wire around itself several times to secure. Tuck the ends of wire under the wrapped bundle (figure C).

figure c

10 Place the organic items you selected (I used strips of dried wood) inside the metal triangle and adhere them with two-part epoxy glue. Hang the pendant from a cord of your choice to finish the necklace.

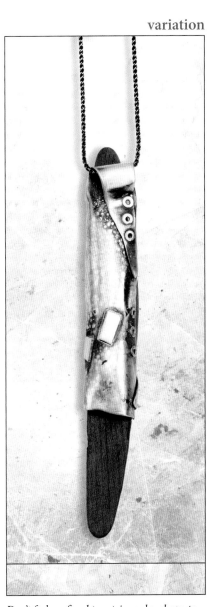

Don't feel confined to a triangular shape to hold your treasures, but keep in mind that it's a good idea to cut shapes from paper, and practice folding them around your object before you head for the metal.

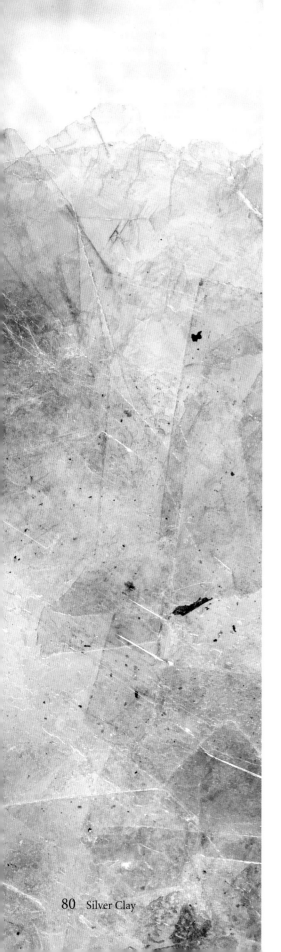

silver clay

Silver clay takes the stage in the next five projects, where you'll learn how to combine clay with sheet metal to create fabulous wearable art. The collection of projects allows you to quickly immerse yourself in tricks of the trade: incorporating wire, sheet metal clay, screen, and mesh will be part of the fun. Don't worry about losing the metalsmithing skills you just learned; you'll simply expand on them.

A new material or technique is added to the silver clay in each project, increasing your range of skills and design options. Due to both the organic quality of the clay and the variations in metals, results will vary by the hands of each artist. This is a great thing!

In the first project, Interweave Pendant, copper wire and sheet metal clay are woven together to create a simple surface design. Captured wires extend from the edges and are balled at the ends, resulting in a quirky, contemporary vibe.

The Perforation Pendant gives the illusion of a cold connection rivet. In this spinning project, a copper disk is pierced with an awl to create holes, then embedded into silver clay. The clay appears through the holes, creating small silver dots.

The next project, Window Brooch, is one of my favorite jacket lapel brooches. Silver clay is extruded through a center square, and the entire piece is framed with detailed stitching.

With Silver Screen Earrings, woven silver mesh allows you to create an unusual texture that resembles tiny fish scales. Screens and mesh are available in a variety of sizes, and you'll enjoy experimenting with the range of textures they produce.

The final project in this series, Lattice Bead Bracelet, brings you back to silver sheet clay, but this time it's woven onto the surface of a large dome bead, also made from silver clay. A simple elastic cord and your choice of accompanying beads complete this reversible design.

As you work with the silver clay, you'll realize the sculptural quality and wonderful range of the material. You'll begin to stretch its limits by integrating your own found objects, trying different weaves, pulling the clay into unusual shapes, and making many other new discoveries.

techniques
Basic metal clay work
Weaving
Balling wire
Adding patina

materials
Silver clay,
Art Clay slow-dry or
PMC+, 0.4 ounce (10 g)

Silver metal slip in syringe in
corresponding brand

Copper wire, 22 gauge,
12 inches (30.5 cm)

Sheet metal clay,
approximately
1 to 2 x ¼ to ½ inches
(2.5 to 5.1 x 0.6 to 1.3 cm)

Liver of sulfur
or commercial black patina

tools
Metal clay kit, page 41
Metal snips

With silver clay as the base of your pendant, you'll build a wonderfully textured surface by weaving copper wire through thin strips of sheet metal clay. Trying different shapes, adding wire, or changing other small details will take you on an amazing creative journey.

interweave pendant

step by step

1 Place a 0.4-ounce (10 g) lump of silver clay on your work surface, and roll a slab that is three playing cards thick.

2 With the craft knife, cut the clay into a long rectangular shape, approximately 2¼ x ½ inches (5.7 x 1.3 cm) (figure A). This form will be the base of the pendant; the bottom can be cut organically or straight. Using your fingers, roll the top of the piece forward onto itself to make a bail. Using the syringe, secure the roll in place with slip (figures B and C).

3 Use metal snips to cut approximately 10 to 12 pieces of 22-gauge wire, each approximately 2 inches (5.1 cm) long. Set these pieces aside. Using the craft knife, cut a piece of sheet metal clay to extend over the top of the bail and down the front of the pendant. Beginning at the bottom of the sheet metal clay piece, make three to five cuts up towards the top edge of the sheet, but not all the way. Stop about ¼-inch (6 mm) from the top edge. You will weave the copper wire into these strips. Place the uncut end of the sheet metal clay on top of the bail (photo 1).

4 Brush the top of the bail with a small amount of water, just enough to moisten it. Gently guide the cut strips towards the base of the piece, spreading them out to make weaving easier (photo 2).

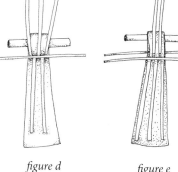

2

5 Beginning at the top of the pendant, just under the bail, and working right to left, pull up every other sheet metal clay strip and slide in a piece of 22-gauge wire. Push the wire as close as you can to the bail (figure D). Lay those strips down over the wire. On the next row, gently pull up the opposite strips, and insert a second wire under them. Scoot the wire close to the one above it (figure E). Continue weaving all the way down the piece, using as many wires as you desire.

figure a

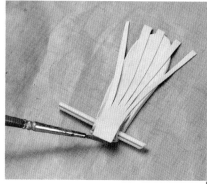

1

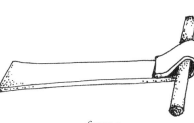

figure b

figure c

figure d

figure e

6 After weaving, lay the strips gently in place. Because nothing has been secured at this point, make sure all the elements are placed exactly where you want them. Then use a small paintbrush to gently dab water over the woven grid, making sure to saturate the entire area (photo 3). The sheet metal clay is very soft at this stage, and the grid will fall apart if too much water is applied or if pressure is put on the surface. Wait for the entire piece to dry.

7 Fire the pendant following the clay's recommended firing schedule. Burn balls on the ends of the extended copper wires. Use a brass brush to clean the piece, and then patina the surface with liver of sulfur or commercial black patina. Let the pendant dry. The brass brush can be used again to remove the black areas on higher surfaces. I like to use my bench grinder to buff the high area to a nice shine. The recessed areas will remain black, creating additional texture and dimension on the surface.

8 Thread a necklace cord or chain through the bail.

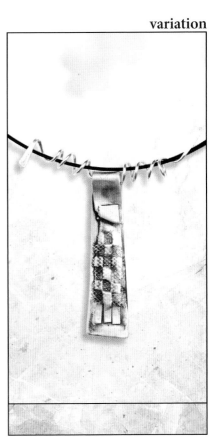

variation

Instead of copper wires, try using strips of sheet metal clay as the base, as well as your weaving material.

3

perforation pendant

the combination of copper sheet metal and silver clay in this pendant is one of my favorites. I love the way the clay creates a riveted appearance on the copper, and the organic edge looks perfectly natural. Allowing the disk to spin freely gives this piece movement and personality.

step by step

1 Wearing safety glasses, use metal snips to cut the copper sheet into a disk 1½ to 2 inches (3.8 to 5.1 cm) in diameter. Anneal and patina the disk with the propane torch. Use the hammer and steel block or anvil to forge the edges, creating a deckled effect. Punch a hole in the center of the disk by hammering the awl into the surface. Use this technique to poke multiple holes throughout the surface of the disk in a random pattern. If you turn the piece over, you'll notice that the openings are very rough.

2 Gently hammer the rough areas on the back of the disk, but do not flatten them. Simply reduce the sharpness; they will protrude but won't be as pointed.

3 Place a 0.4-ounce (10 g) lump of silver clay on your surface, and roll it the width of four playing cards. Place the copper disk on top of the clay. Use the craft knife to cut around the disk in an organic shape, leaving about ⅛ to ¼ inch (3 to 6 mm) of clay extending beyond the perimeter (figure A). Set aside any remaining clay, and keep it moist.

4 With your fingers, gently roll the edges of the clay up and around the perimeter of the disk, securing it in place. Pick the piece up, and carefully push the clay through the holes on the back of the disk until a small amount pokes through the front surface. Pat the clay dots that poked through the front surface until they are flat (photo 1).

1

5 Scratch small indentions into the clay edge with a ballpoint pen to create texture (figure B). With the awl, bore the clay out of the center hole where the necklace will hang.

6 Roll the remaining silver clay into a ball, then flatten it with the plastic roller to the thickness of three playing cards, leaving the edges organic and irregular. Apply a rubber stamp to the surface of this piece to create texture.

7 Fire the large disk and the smaller silver clay piece together, following the clay's recommended firing schedule. Remove the pieces from the kiln, and quench or cool them. Use a brass brush to clean both pieces. Apply liver of sulfur or commercial black patina to the silver clay portion of the large disk and to the smaller silver clay piece. Buff them to remove any blackness from the higher surfaces of the pattern. The pieces are now ready to assemble.

8 Stack the small silver clay piece on top of the large disk. For a nice finishing detail, add small flat beads to the front and back. Thread the series of beads onto the wire. Measure about a third of the way down the 4- to 5-inch (10.2 to 12.7 cm) piece of sterling wire, and at that point, use pliers to bend the wire into a 90° angle (figure C).

figure a

figure b

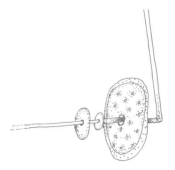

figure c

perforation pendant

9 Measure about ⅛ to ¼ inch (3 to 6 mm) from the first bend in the wire, and now bend the other side. This will leave a little extra space where your beads hang, giving them room to rotate and swing.

10 Finish the pendant by making a wrapped loop on the first connection. If you desire, add a bead before the final wrapped loop is made (figures D and E). Thread a necklace cord or chain through the loop.

figure d

figure e

variation

If you'd like to experiment by changing the type of clay or sheet metal used in a project, this pendant is a great place to start. Fire several beads using a variety of clays and shapes, and test them with different sheet metal colors before you fully commit to your design.

window brooch

the perfect accessory for a man's suit jacket, this geometric broach is easy to learn and fun to construct. Copper sheets make a great background for extruded silver clay, and the stitched border provides a simple, but eye-catching frame.

window brooch

step by step

1 Prepare the square copper background by cutting two copper sheets, each approximately 1½ to 2 inches (3.8 to 5.1 cm) square. Using the propane torch and wearing safety glasses, patina the copper pieces one at a time.

2 Set one of the copper squares onto a scrap piece of hard wood and prepare to cut a square window into the center. Place the sharp end of the flathead screwdriver where you would like to create one edge of the window. Hammer on the handle of the screwdriver to cut into the copper. Gradually move the screwdriver along the area you want cut open, making a square window frame (photo 1). The size of the frame is up to you. When you have completed the cuts, remove the inside copper piece.

3 Using the hammer and steel block or anvil, forge the inner and outer edges of the copper pieces to create a deckled effect and a smooth texture. File or cut any sharp edges until they are smooth.

4 Set aside a piece of copper screen that is a little smaller than the outer perimeter of the copper square frame. Roll approximately 0.1 ounces (2 g) of silver clay into a ball between your fingers. Slowly begin to push it through the screen. Make sure as you continue to push that you leave plenty of clay on the backside of the screen. Don't push it all the way through (photo 2).

5 Place the cut piece of copper over the extruded clay, and gently press it down so the clay comes up through the window. Gently spread apart the small clay strips that poked through the screen, allowing some to grab the edges of the window (photo 3).

2

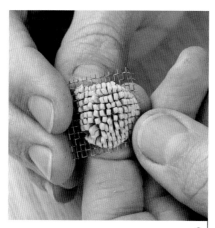

1

6 Fire this piece in the kiln at the clay's recommended firing schedule. After removing the piece from the kiln, let it cool and brush the extruded silver with a brass brush.

7 Apply liver of sulfur or commercial black patina to the silver clay and buff it to bring the shine back. With the hole punch, puncture two holes in each corner of the copper frame. Use these holes as a pattern to punch holes in the other copper square piece (figure A). This will be the back of the brooch.

8 With a jeweler's saw or sharp screwdriver, cut two small squares on the uncut copper square for the pin back (figure B). Slide the pin into place before assembling the brooch (figure C).

9 Cut the 10-inch (25.4 cm) piece of 20-gauge wire into four pieces, each about the same length. Hammer the ends of each piece to look like paddles.

10 Place the copper squares on top of each other with the holes lining up and the silver protrusion facing up through the window. Burn a ball on one end of the 26-gauge stitching wire. Thread it through one set of holes, back to front, and anchor it by stitching it back through the same hole (figure D).

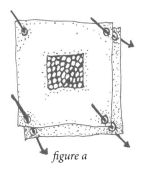

figure a

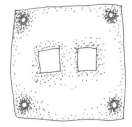

figure b

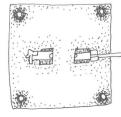

figure c

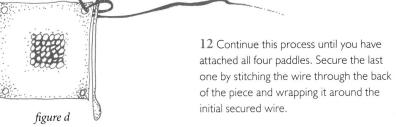

figure d

11 Place one paddle next to the edge where you began stitching. Begin connecting the paddle to the edge by wrapping the wire around it towards the other end (photo 4). Wrap the wire tight at first, and then spread the coils apart as you work towards the end of the paddle. Near the other end, wrap the coils tight again as you come to the next connection. Stitch the wire into the next holes, around the corner, and up through the following holes to add a second paddle.

4

12 Continue this process until you have attached all four paddles. Secure the last one by stitching the wire through the back of the piece and wrapping it around the initial secured wire.

Silver Clay **89**

silver screen earrings

design beautiful, simple earrings with silver mesh and silver clay. Mesh is a fantastic material to combine with clay because it fires beautifully and takes on a lovely sheen and texture when embedded. I frequently use mesh to enhance the surfaces of my jewelry—the material has such potential!

step by step

1 Determine the shape and size of the earrings you would like to create. The smaller version featured here is ½ x ¾ inch (1.3 x 1.9 cm), and the larger version is ½ x 1½ inches (1.3 x 3.8 cm). Cut two pieces of silver mesh into the shape and size you selected. Bend the edges of the mesh backwards to help attach them to the clay.

2 Place a 0.4-ounce (10 g) lump of silver clay on your work surface, and roll it to the width of three playing cards. Use the craft knife to cut the clay into the same shape as your mesh; the clay should be approximately ⅛ inch (3 mm) bigger than the mesh on all sides. Place the mesh on the clay with the bent edges touching first (photo 1). Adhere the mesh to the clay by rolling it with the plastic roller (photo 2).

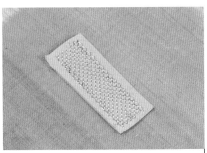

1

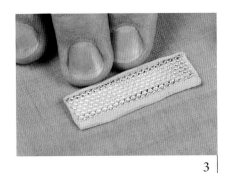

2

3 Once the mesh is secured, gently pull the sides of the clay up over the edges of the mesh. Slightly roll the lips of the clay to create a secure hold (photo 3).

3

4 Poke a hole through the top of each earring with a small straw. You will later insert ear hooks through these holes.

5 Fire the earrings following the clay's recommended firing schedule. After removing the pieces from the kiln, either shine them with a brass brush or buff them with the de-burring wheel on the grinder. Liver of sulfur or commercial black patina can be applied to darken the piece; when buffed, it will add dimension and depth.

6 Attach ear hooks of your choice.

variation

The Silver Screen Earrings can easily be converted to pendants. For a little variety, try using brass screen or stainless mesh. An additional piece of sheet metal can serve as a backdrop to the pendant, as shown here.

lattice bead bracelet

materials
Silver clay, Art Clay
slow-dry or PMC+,
0.4 ounces (10 g)

Sheet metal clay,
approximately
$1\frac{1}{2}$ x $1\frac{1}{2}$ inches
(3.8 x 3.8 cm)

Silver metal slip in syringe

Elastic cord, 8 to 9 inches
(20.3 to 22.9 cm)

Commercial bead
assortment

Liver of sulfur
or commercial black patina

tools
Metal clay kit, page 41
Plastic circle template
2 light bulbs

this piece is all about the focal point. Using silver clay to make a large bead with a woven surface, your bracelet will truly stand out. Keep in mind, the bead can also be hung low on a necklace or easily featured on a choker for a nice statement. In this project, you'll create a simple bracelet with a focal bead surrounded by smaller accent beads on a cord.

step by step

1 Place a 0.4-ounce (10 g) lump of silver clay on your work surface, and roll a slab that is three playing cards thick. Select a circle size from the plastic circle template, and place that circle on the rolled clay. Cut out the circle with the craft knife. This circle will become the top half of your bead. You'll make the back half a little later.

2 Cut small indentions on opposite sides of the circle. The indentions will later become a hole through which you will string the cord. Gently lay the circle on a light bulb. Make sure the entire clay circle is touching the bulb and is evenly placed (photo 1).

3 Cut a piece of sheet metal clay to fit the circle, approximately ¾ x 1 inch (1.9 x 2.5 cm). Cut into the ¾-inch (1.9 cm) side, creating four to five strips. Don't cut all the way through the other side, but leave the strips held together by ¼ inch (6 mm) of sheet metal clay on the end. It will have the appearance of fringe (figure A). Set this piece aside. Now cut five to seven individual strips of sheet metal clay, approximately 1 inch (2.5 cm) or longer to fit your circle. These strips are "weavers" and will be woven into the other strips of sheet metal clay held in place by the uncut end (figure B).

4 Wet the paintbrush with a small amount of water. Gently paint or dab water on a side of the clay circle that does not have an indention. Attach the uncut end of the sheet metal clay piece by placing it on the wet area. Gently spread apart the strips (photo 2).

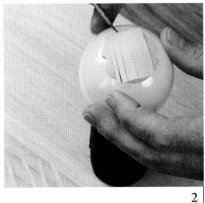

2

5 Insert the first weaver by pulling up every other strip of the anchored sheet metal clay strips and carefully weaving it through them (figure C). Lay the top layers down over the weaver.

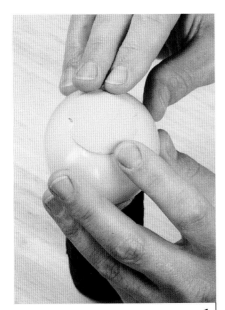

1

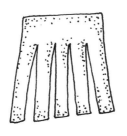

figure a

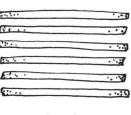

figure b

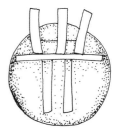

figure c

6 Begin the next row. Insert the second weaver by again lifting up every other strip of anchored sheet metal clay strips. This time, lift opposite strips to create the checkerboard pattern (figure D). Continue in this fashion until all five to seven weavers are inserted and the weave is tight (figure E).

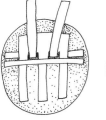 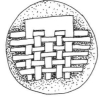

figure d   *figure e*

7 When all the weavers are in place, approximately 1/8 inch (3 mm) of space should remain on the ends of the anchored sheet metal clay strips. Very gently dab a small amount of water over the entire woven area. The clay is very fragile at this stage and will break if too much water or pressure is applied. This process will secure the sheet metal clay to the silver clay circle. Dry the dome on the light bulb.

8 Follow steps 1 through 7 to create the other half of the bead. Be creative! This side of the bead can be woven, but you may decide to create a different pattern or create texture with a rubber stamp.

9 After both domes are dry, smooth the backs of the circles with sandpaper (photos 3 and 4).

10 Assemble the bead. With the syringe, squeeze silver metal slip around the edge of one circle without covering the indentions (photo 5). Place the other circle on top of it. If you notice any gaps in the connection, squeeze some of the silver metal slip into the area. Press and smooth the soft clay seam. Dry the bead.

11 Smooth the connecting seam of the bead with sandpaper. Fire the bead following the clay's recommended firing schedule. Remove the bead from the kiln and clean it with the brass brush. Apply liver of sulfur or commercial black patina to the bead. Finish by buffing the surface again to remove blackness from the higher parts of the pattern.

12 String your assortment of commercial beads on the elastic cord with the large focal bead in the center. Tie a knot in the cord to secure the beads, and hide the knot by tucking it into the large bead.

variation

Use a variety of wires, beads, and other techniques or clays to alter the bracelet. By applying a different texture to each side, it becomes reversible.

3

4

5

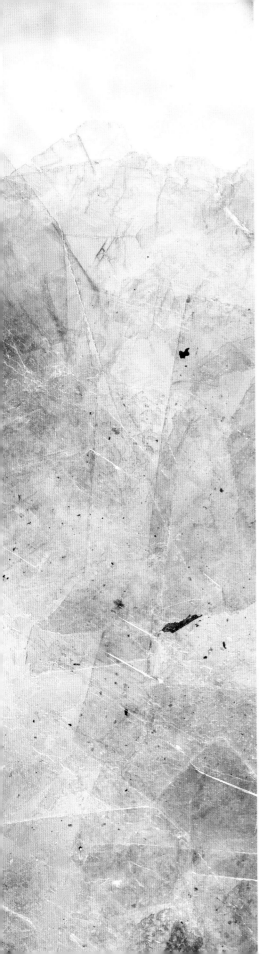

bronze clay

Shifting from silver to bronze clay, you'll experience new, rich tones and beautiful colorations that mix well with copper, silver, brass, and galvanized metal combinations. Bronze clay, unlike silver, takes a long time to fire in the kiln. It needs to heat up slowly and hold a higher temperature for a longer period of time. The moment you remove a fired bronze piece from the kiln, you'll know the extra time was well worth the wait.

We begin this section with a dangling Confetti Bracelet that uses two styles of clay beads: small flat disks and larger circular forms. I let color remain on the beads after firing because they resemble confetti when assembled with silver wire accents. I'm a firm believer that it's always good to have confetti on hand!

The Gridlock Brooch utilizes a great find from the hardware store. Galvanized metal cloth is a strong, dull silver material used in fencing and manufacturing applications. I use it as a structure for the clay, but the grid also becomes a primary design element. You'll love how the clay pulls away from the metal and leaves a jagged, industrial form.

The next two projects involve simple slab work. In Bronze Quiver Pendant, a stamped rectangle is shaped into a pocket for holding long strips of copper wire. This piece is then stitched to a copper sheet metal base. With Bronze & Copper Bangles, clay is draped around heavy-gauge copper wire, and wrapped in an organic, twisted fashion. Because of its great moisture, bronze happens to be the easiest of the metal clays to drape and shape. This bracelet is by far the easiest project in the book.

The last bronze project in this section is a Stitched Triangle Pendant. Here, you'll join three bronze pieces together with tied wires, and add copper paddles to the edges with wrapped wires.

Bronze clay is an amazing product to play with, and it produces gorgeous jewelry. I suggest that you experiment with the surface and enjoy the variety of results that can be achieved from leaving the colors just as they appear out of the kiln versus polishing them to a shine. Bronze clay is extremely strong after firing and will give you long-lasting jewelry that only looks better with age.

This bronze bead bracelet is a party on your wrist. Shaped into multiple sizes, stamped with texture, and connected by a cluster of jump rings, it's fun to make and more fun to wear.

techniques

Basic metal clay work

Stamping

Wirework

materials

Bronze clay,
1.1 ounces (30 grams)

Sterling silver wire,
20 gauge, 30 inches
(76.2 cm)

26 to 30 small crystal beads

60 to 75 silver jump rings,
16 to 18 gauge,
4 to 5 mm in diameter

Silver toggle clasp

tools

Metal clay kit, page 41

Coal or coconut carbon

Stainless steel container

Two pairs
of needle-nose pliers

Round-nose pliers

step by step

1 Place a 0.4-ounce (10 g) lump of bronze clay on your work surface, and roll a slab that is two to three playing cards thick. Make about 30 beads by cutting circles into the clay with the large straw. Insert the small straw into each circle bead, making a small hole in each (photo 1). Dry the beads.

1

2 Apply oil or lubricating gel to the scrapbooking stamp to prevent sticking. Roll a small amount of clay between your fingers to create a ball. Gently push the clay onto the stamp, and press it with your thumb (photo 2). Remove the clay from the stamp. Insert the small straw into the clay bead to make a small hole. Repeat this process for 25 to 30 charm beads. Allow them to dry.

2

3 Fire all the beads following the clay's recommended firing schedule. Remove the beads from the kiln. Begin the process of placing wrapped loops on each bead and adding the small crystal beads to each wire as follows.

Place a wrapped loop on a disk bead by inserting a 3-inch (7.6 cm) piece of wire about a third of the way through the hole in the bead (figure A).

figure a

Bend the short side of the wire up, and wrap it approximately three times to secure it around the longer extending wire (figure B).

figure b

confetti bracelet

Thread a small circular bronze bead and a small crystal bead onto the wire (figure C).

figure c

Make another wrapped loop, this time twisting it back down around the wire toward the crystal bead (figure D).

figure d

4 Begin assembling the bracelet. Attach three jump rings to the circular portion of the toggle clasp. On the second jump ring, add a beaded wrapped loop wire. On the third jump ring, add a small circular bronze bead (figure E).

figure e

If you prefer a shiny bracelet, you may choose to polish the beads after firing, as shown above. To achieve the coloration of the featured project, simply assemble the bracelet immediately after removing the beads from the kiln.

5 As shown in figure F, continue the process in step 4. On every third addition of the beaded wrapped loop wire, add a jump ring to the top of the wrapped loop to lengthen it. Continue steps 4 and 5 to the desired length of your bracelet.

figure f

6 Attach the toggle clasp bar with a jump ring. Use two pliers to separate the jump ring to the side. (Opening the circle by pulling it apart can change the shape and weaken the jump ring.) Close the jump ring using the same method (photo 3).

3

gridlock brooch

the unpredictability of this project makes it my favorite! Using wire or galvanized wire cloth as a grid holding bronze clay, you'll discover wonderful variations in texture, content, and color. After firing, the grid sometimes separates from the clay, the wire might break, or holes and rips may appear in the structure. It's all part of the fun!

step by step

1 Cut the galvanized wire grid into the desired shape. The wire grid for the brooch featured here is 6 x 6 squares. With metal snips, clip off any sharp, protruding points along the edges. Use a metal file or bench grinder to smooth the edges until they form a solid line.

2 Place a 0.4-ounce (10 g) lump of bronze clay on your work surface, and roll a slab that is three playing cards thick. Place the grid on top of the clay, but do not press or roll it yet. Use the grid as a guide to cut the bronze clay approximately ⅛ inch (3 mm) larger than the grid on all sides. With the plastic roller, press the grid into the clay (photo 1).

3 Cut the clay around the edge of the grid, just enough to secure the screen. Fire the piece according to the bronze clay recommendation. You will notice the clay has shrunk from firing. This leaves wonderful gaps and edges that pull away from the screen. I often remove a loose square to leave a hole in the piece.

4 Set the grid aside, and anneal the copper sheet. Texture the copper with a hammer, and deckle the edges to create an organic shape. Use a powdered cleanser and steel wool to remove carbon and dirt from the back of the piece. You may also use a pickle to clean the surface. Solder the pin back onto the copper piece (see page 45).

5 Assemble the brooch by dividing the 26-gauge wire into four equal lengths, each approximately 4 inches (10.2 cm). Burn a ball on one end of each wire. If the clay has pulled away from the edge of the screen, use this space to insert the wire. Otherwise, drill a small hole in the corner.

1

6 Use the wire placements as a template to punch or drill four holes in the copper sheet. Thread the wire from the front to back of the brooch, resting the ball on top of the grid. Bring the wire from the back of the brooch, around the edge, and to the front. Insert it back into the hole. Repeat this process for each corner (figure A).

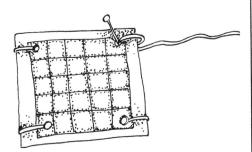

figure a

7 On the back of the brooch, secure the wires by looping them under the existing pieces. Repeat the loops a couple of times, and then cut them close. Repeat this process for each corner to complete the project (figure B).

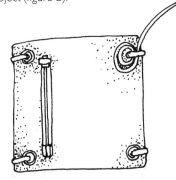

figure b

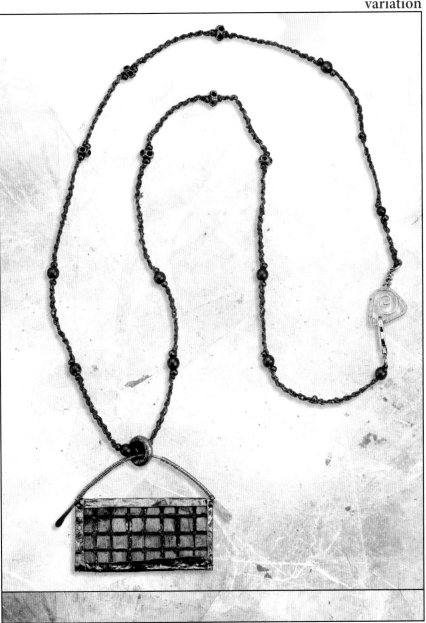

I easily converted the gridlock brooch into a pendant cased in copper foil with .002 thickness. Simply attach a silver wire paddle to the top corners with copper wire wrapping, and use a large accent bead for the hanger.

bronze quiver pendant

Stitched along the seams and holding a bundle of wire, this pendant offers great impact without being too difficult to create—it's really just stamping, balling, and stitching! Leave the clay a natural color, as it appears right out of the hot kiln, to give the impression of raku pottery.

step by step

1 With metal snips, cut the copper sheet into an oblong piece, 1 x 3 inches (2.5 x 7.6 cm). Anneal the copper with the propane torch, and round the corners with metal snips. Hammer the edges to create a deckled effect, or use the bench grinder to smooth them. This piece is the pendant's base.

2 Place a 0.4- to 0.5-ounce (10 to 15 g) lump of bronze clay on your work surface, and roll a slab that is three playing cards thick. Use the rubber stamp to apply texture to the clay. Gently remove the clay from the stamp, and lay it over a ballpoint pen. With the pen intact, lay the clay over the copper base, and spread the long edges of the clay over it. The pen stays in place until the clay is dry (figure A). Using scrap clay and the craft knife, cut a small rectangle, approximately 1/4 x 1 1/2 inches (6 mm x 3.8 cm). This piece will become the top hanger (figure B).

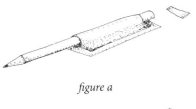

figure a

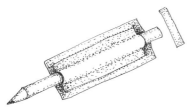

figure b

3 With the craft knife, cut the edges of the clay to match the long sides of the copper base (photo 1). Cut the top and bottom edges so that 1/4 inch (6 mm) of the base is revealed at both ends. After both pieces dry, remove the pen and fire the pieces following the clay's recommended firing schedule. Remove them from the kiln.

1

4 Using a 1/16-inch (1.6 mm) bit, or 1/16-inch (1.6 mm) hole punch, drill or puncture eight holes into each long side of the fired clay pendant (photo 2). Use these holes as a pattern for drilling holes into the copper base. Lay the bronze clay piece on top of the copper base so the holes match up. You're ready to stitch the pieces together.

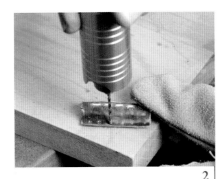

2

5 Burn a ball on each end of the 24-inch (70 cm) piece of 26-gauge copper wire. Cut the wire in half. Thread one wire, front to back, through the top hole on the left side of the pendant so the ball catches at the top. Go through both the clay and copper base layers. Perform a reverse blanket-stitch along the edge, catching the stitches on the back of the pendant as you go (figure C).

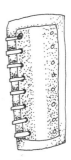

figure c

6 When you reach the end of the left side, secure the wire on the back of the piece by tucking it under the last stitch a couple of times and cutting it close (figure D).

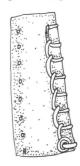

figure d

bronze quiver pendant

7 Cut about 8 to 12 pieces of the 18-gauge copper wire. Vary the lengths anywhere between 3 and 5 inches (7.6 and 12.7 cm). Burn balls on both ends of each piece. Tie the bundle together with wire as shown in figure E, and push it into the arch between the top of the pendant and the base. Bundle enough wire to create a tight fit that won't slide.

figure e

8 Follow steps 5 and 6 to blanket-stitch the other side of the pendant, securing the bundle of wire in place (figures F and G).

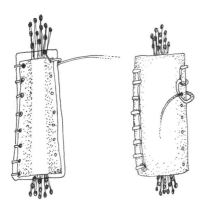

figure f　　　　*figure g*

9 Drill holes into the top of the copper base on each side of the wire bundle. Lay the small rectangular clay bar horizontally about ¼ inch (6 mm) above the bundle. Drill two holes into the bar, straight up from the holes in the copper base. With 18-gauge copper wire, make two wrapped loops coming out of each hole on the base.

10 Bring the wires up and attach them to the rectangular bar, again with wrapped loops (figure H).

11 Drill two more holes in the corners of the bronze bar and attach the neck chain.

figure h

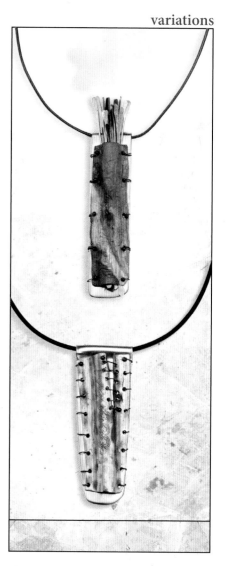

If you like to experiment, this is the project for you! Make the copper base longer, and roll it back to create a hanger. Add an intentional repair to the bronze clay by cutting it before it dries, and stitching it back together after the piece is fired. Try using silver or brass sheets for the base or use paddles for the bundle instead of balled wire.

bronze & copper bangles

techniques
Wirework
Basic metal clay work

materials
Copper wire,
14 or 16 gauge,
30 inches (76.2 cm)
Bronze clay,
1.1 ounces (30 g)

tools
Metal clay kit, page 41
Round-nose pliers
Metal snips
Metal file
Ballpoint pen or awl
Coal or coconut carbon
Stainless steel container

Using heavy gauge copper wire and a simple rolling technique, these bracelets may be the simplest project in the book. They're fun, fast, and yield beautiful results reminiscent of ancient Roman jewels.

step by step

1 Beginning in the center of the 30-inch (76.2 cm) piece of copper wire, wrap a circle twice around your wrist to measure the size of your bracelet. Clay will be wrapped around the wire later, so the bracelet must be slightly bigger than you would usually wear.

2 Remove the wire from your wrist. Measure 4 inches (10.2 cm) from one end of the wire, and wrap the end once around the bracelet. Then wrap the very end of the remaining wire around the bracelet, either coiling it close together or leaving space between wires. If there is a little space between the wraps, the clay will better adhere during the firing and shrinking process.

3 Repeat step 2 to wrap the other end of the wire. Cut both wires so the tips are flush with the bracelet (photo 1). Smooth them with the metal file or bench grinder.

4 Roll 0.5 ounces (15 g) of bronze clay between your fingers to make it soft and warm, then roll it on the nonstick surface with your fingers. Spread your fingers apart so the roll of clay is not uniform. Roll a length of about 5 to 8 inches (12.7 to 20.3 cm) (photo 2).

5 At the center of the roll, loop the clay over the wire bracelet. Wrap one end of the roll tight around the wire in an open wrap (photo 3). Then wrap the other side of the roll in the same fashion. If the clay breaks, begin wrapping again in the same location.

1

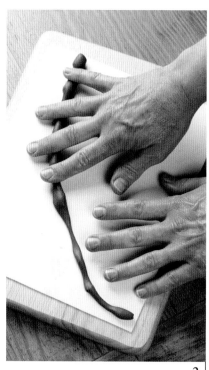

2

3

6 Roll the remaining 0.5 ounces (15 g) of bronze clay and repeat steps 4 and 5 to finish the wrap (photo 4). Handle the bracelet gently, so the clay does not separate from the wire. If desired, texture the clay with holes by using a ballpoint pen or awl. Rather than heating the bracelet, allow it to air dry. The clay better adheres to the metal when dried naturally.

4

7 Fire the bracelet according to the clay's recommended firing schedule. For an aged look with a matte finish, as shown in the featured project, do not polish the bracelet after it is removed from the kiln.

variation

If your taste is a little more chic, polish the bracelet with the brass brush after firing it, and wrap 22-gauge copper wire around the surface for further embellishment.

this project is the perfect canvas if you love working with color. The amazing hues of fired bronze clay are incorporated into other design elements within the pendant. Copper wire-wrapped paddles frame the piece and beautifully set off the clay's smoky blue, green, and red tones.

techniques

Basic metal clay work

Wirework

Weaving

Balling wire

materials

Bronze clay, 0.2 to 0.4 ounces (5 to10 g)

Copper wire, 18 gauge, 24 to 30 inches (70 to 76.2 cm)

Copper wire, 26 gauge, 36 inches (91.4 cm)

tools

Metal clay kit, page 41

Coal or coconut carbon

Stainless steel container

Drill with $1/16$-inch (1.6 mm) bit, or $1/16$-inch (1.6 mm) hole punch

Metal snips

Hammer

Block of scrap wood

Round-nose pliers

step by step

1 Place a 0.4-ounce (10 g) lump of bronze clay on your work surface, and roll a slab that is three playing cards thick.

2 Use the stamp to cover the clay with impressions. With the craft knife, cut several long strips from the stamped clay, each approximately 2 x $1/4$ inches (5.1 x 0.6 cm). I slightly vary the length and width of each piece, and leave the ends natural. With scrap clay, make two to three disk beads by cutting the clay with the large straw and making a small hole in the bead with the small straw. Dry all the pieces (photo 1).

1

3 Fire three triangular strips and the beads following the clay's recommended firing schedule. Remove the pieces from the kiln and arrange the three strips into a triangle with overlapping ends. Do not brush, sand, or buff the surface. Instead, allow the kiln-fired color to become a design element. Drill holes at both ends of each piece.

4 Each side of the triangle will be framed by two paddles. Cut five pieces of 18-gauge copper wire, each approximately 2½ inches (6.4 cm). The wires should be long enough to extend about $1/4$ inch (6 mm) beyond the triangle's edges, but they can vary slightly in length. Cut another piece of 18-gauge copper wire approximately 8 inches (20.3 cm). This piece will become the hanger.

5 Hammer paddles on the ends of the five short copper wires. On the long wire, only hammer one end, because you'll be using the other end to create a wrapped loop.

6 Cut the 26-gauge copper wire into three pieces, each approximately 12 inches (30.5 cm) long. Burn a ball on one end of each length. Thread each wire through the overlapping holes at the corners of the triangle, with the balls resting on top. Pull the wires snug to hold the pieces together. Loop the wires back through the holes to secure them (photo 2).

2

7 Lay one pair of the short paddles flat against the left edge of the triangle, and begin wrapping the paddles with the loose wire. Secure them together with a tightly coiled under/over weave.

8 When you reach the end of the bronze edge, thread the wire into the top hole of the triangle, and tuck it under the wire on the back.

9 Repeat the wrapping process, adding the long 8-inch (20.3 cm) paddle and a short paddle at the top of the triangle (photo 3). Now, two sets of paddles are secured, and two edges are framed.

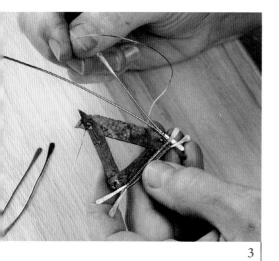

3

variation

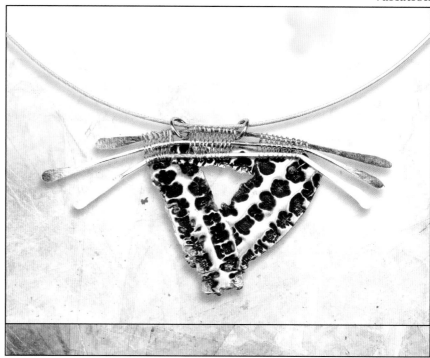

Irregular edges and shapes can add texture to the triangle. Try a version of this pendant using silver clay with rough edges, and add three paddled bars to the top edge only, as shown here.

10 On the final edge of the triangle, add the last pair of short paddles. Weave and secure the last two paddles in the same fashion as the others.

11 Thread the disk beads onto the long wire extending from the top of the triangle, and finish the top with a simple wrapped loop. Thread a neck chain through the hanger to complete the necklace (figure A). The cord shown here is a copper colored rubber cord.

figure a

copper clay

The following five projects introduce copper clay, and teach you how to combine the material with wire and other metals. As the newest metal clay on the market, information about it is constantly being updated, and jewelers and artists are just beginning to realize its possibilities. Consider this an exciting time of discovery.

I quickly realized that copper clay really speaks to me for a number of reasons. It's not only beautiful, but also has a faster firing time than bronze; it's softer and easier to work with; and its post-firing color applications are more varied than any other metal clay.

The first project, Relic Pendant, presents torn copper clay as a surface decoration resting on hinged silver sheet metal. Learning to connect pieces with hinges will carry you a long way in jewelry making, and you'll love the movement they generate.

The Copper Vessel Pendant is constructed from triangle slabs fused together with slip. Because the clay is very moist, joining pieces to create three-dimensional objects works quite well.

The next project, Draped Copper Trio, uses simple rolled copper beads to make a jewelry set. A bracelet, earrings, and necklace are all fired together and assembled quickly. After making the beads, you can connect them with jump rings, use them for stringing, or in conjunction with chain mail and other complementary beads.

The fourth project, Figure Study, is probably the quirkiest one in the book. Let your creativity take over as you design figurative shapes by simply cutting them out with a craft knife. Body parts are assembled with wrapped wire loops or jump rings, and found objects can represent arms, legs, or other parts of the figure. Accessorize your little person with beads and metal scraps or findings.

We finish the book with a simple Copper Ring project that yields stunning results. A small piece of draped copper clay forms a ring band, and a stamped ball of clay forms the gem. As with many of the projects, you can make this ring reversible, polish different portions of it, and manipulate the colors. Whatever you decide, it's a quick way to feel great about working with copper clay.

Use the newness of copper clay as a reason to practice fearless experimentation. Even in its infancy, it has already proven to be a product that designers love to work with. So, be bold, have fun, and enjoy the ride.

techniques
Cutting
Forging
Basic metal clay work
Punching or drilling
Balling wire

materials
Silver sheet, 24 gauge,
2 x 4 inches (5.1 x 10.2 cm)

Copper clay, 0.1 to 0.2
ounces (2 to 5 g)

Miniature nuts and bolts
Copper wire, 18 gauge,
12 inches (30.5 cm)

tools
Sheet metal kit, page 41
Metal clay kit, page 41
Coconut carbon
Stainless steel container
Ballpoint pen

the hinges on this pendant give it great movement, while the torn-away clay embellishment on the surface offers a touch of antiquity. You'll apply many basic metal-working techniques with this project that can easily be transferred to earrings or bracelets. Enjoy the possibilities!

step by step

1 From the silver sheet, use metal snips to cut a triangle approximately 3½ inches (8.9 cm) long. The base of the triangle should be 1¼ inches (3.2 cm) wide. Cut the triangle into three sections of equal length (figures A and B).

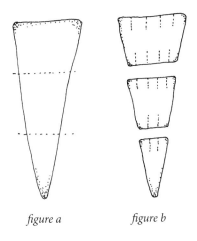

figure a   *figure b*

2 To prepare the hinges, cut ¼-inch (6 mm) tabs. Make four cuts on both edges of the largest section; make four cuts on the long edge of the middle section and two cuts on the short edge; make two cuts on the long edge of the smallest section.

3 Using needle-nose pliers, bend every other tab back and forth until it breaks off (photo 1).

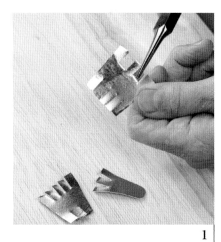

1

4 Hammer the cut edges to achieve rounded, more organic corners. The tabs should fit together like a puzzle (figure C). Because I prefer some movement between the hinges, I cut extra space for each connection. Set these pieces aside.

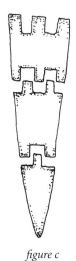

figure c

5 Place 0.1 to 0.2 ounces (2 to 5 g) of copper clay on your work surface, and roll it three playing cards thick. Press the metal print plate or rubber scrapbooking stamp into the clay. Pull the clay away from the stamp or plate and tear it into three shapes that will eventually fit onto the silver segments (photo 2).

2

6 With the awl, mark points in the copper clay where you will later drill holes for the nuts and bolts. I mark four holes in the large piece, three in the medium piece, and two in the small piece. Whatever amount you decide, make sure it's enough to secure the copper pieces to the silver base. Dry the pieces on a flat, nonstick surface. If the edges curl, gently flatten them with your fingers. Fire them following the clay's recommended firing schedule.

7 Remove the pieces from the kiln, and buff them with the brass brush or bench grinder. Attach the three copper clay pieces to the three silver sheets by first punching or drilling 1/16-inch (1.6 mm) holes through the awl marks on the copper.

8 Place the three copper pieces on the three silver sheets, and use the holes as a pattern to punch or drill holes through the silver. Thread the miniature bolts through the copper and silver holes. Using two pliers, screw nuts onto each bolt on the back on the pieces. One pair of pliers holds the bolt and the other tightens the nut. Cut off the excess ends of the bolts with the flush cutter and metal file, or smooth them with the bench grinder. Dab epoxy on each nut connection to assure they will not unscrew.

9 Align the three silver segments so they form the original triangle. Cut a piece of 18-gauge copper wire for each of the three hinges. The top wire should be 1½ inches (3.8 cm) wider than the silver sheet. The two smaller wires should be ½ to 1 inch (1.3 to 2.5 cm) wider than the silver sheet where they will be placed. Burn balls on all six ends of wire. The top wire extends farther out from the sheet than the two smaller wires; they extend just beyond the hinges (figure D).

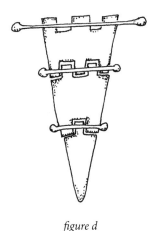

figure d

10 Beginning at the top of the pendant, center the long wire along the silver edge. Gently roll the tabs around the wire, one by one, with needle-nose pliers. When the tabs are even and closed, gently pull the wire up through the spaces between the tabs. Create the other two hinges by rolling each tab into a hook shape with the needle-nose pliers. Insert the copper wires, and tighten the tabs to secure them (photo 3).

3

11 To create a hanger, burn a ball on each end of a 4-inch (10.2 cm) piece of 18-gauge copper wire. Wrap the wire around a ballpoint pen, leaving a 1/16-inch (1.6 mm) space between coils. Thread the coil between the extended wires on the top edge of the piece (figure E). Complete the necklace by stringing a silver neck chain through the copper wire coil.

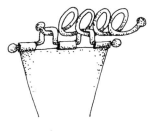

figure e

techniques

Basic metal clay work
Slab building
Wirework (optional)

materials

Triangle patterns
Copper clay,
0.7 ounces (20 g)
Copper wire, 18 gauge,
12 inches (30.5 cm)
(optional)
Copper jump rings
(optional)

tools

Metal clay kit, page 41
Awl
Coconut carbon
Stainless steel container

this simple neckpiece is suitable for both women and men, with its geometric shape and pronounced form. Copper clay looks especially bold, but you may choose other metal clays as desired. I show the piece on a long beaded chain, but you may consider short cords for a more masculine approach.

copper vessel pendant

step by step

1 Use the patterns shown here to cut three elongated triangles from paper. The figure A triangle will become the base of the pendant, and the triangles in figure B will form the front cup.

figure a

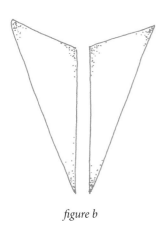

figure b

2 Place a 0.4 ounce (10 g) lump of copper clay on your work surface, and roll a slab that is three playing cards thick. Press the rubber scrapbooking stamp into the clay to create a pattern. Lay the paper triangles gently on the clay, and cut out the shapes with the craft knife. Roll the top edge of the larger triangle over a small straw to make the hanger. The pattern should face forward as you roll the clay towards the back (photo 1).

1|

3 Dry the three triangles before sanding their edges. Place sandpaper on a flat surface, and gently push the clay's edges back and forth against the paper. Collect the shavings and dust for slip that will join the three pieces.

4 Connect the three triangles by painting each seam with a small amount of water. Use the wet paintbrush to mix a diluted slip from dust shavings, and gently dab it into the seams to hold the connection.

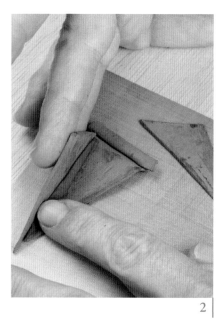

2|

5 Roll 0.1 ounces (2 g) of soft clay into three long, thin pieces, each matching the length of the seams. Place the rolls on the inner seams of the triangle, and gently push the clay into the crevices and corners of each seam to seal it (photo 2). Use an awl or long tool to push the clay into the inner corners.

6 With the wet paintbrush, smooth the seams on the outside, and dry the piece. Add more slip made from dust and water (photo 3).

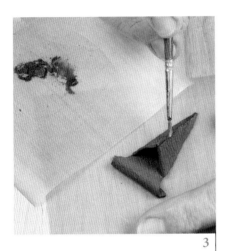

3

7 If any seams need repair, add more slip, smooth, and re-dry the piece. It can be filed or sanded again if you notice any rough edges.

8 Fire the pendant following the clay's recommended firing schedule. After the piece has been removed from the kiln and cooled, smooth it with the brass brush. Clean the copper with the bench grinder and polish.

9 Finish the necklace by threading a neck chain through the pendant's hanger. You may also insert 18-gauge copper wire through the hanger and create wrapped loops on each end. Add jump rings to the wrapped loops, and attach a handmade chain.

variation

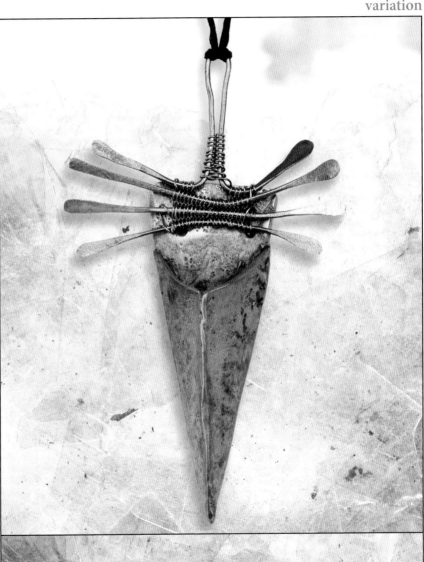

Experiment with an assortment of hangers like the connected copper paddles shown here. Refrain from buffing all the patina off the copper to achieve a muted green color.

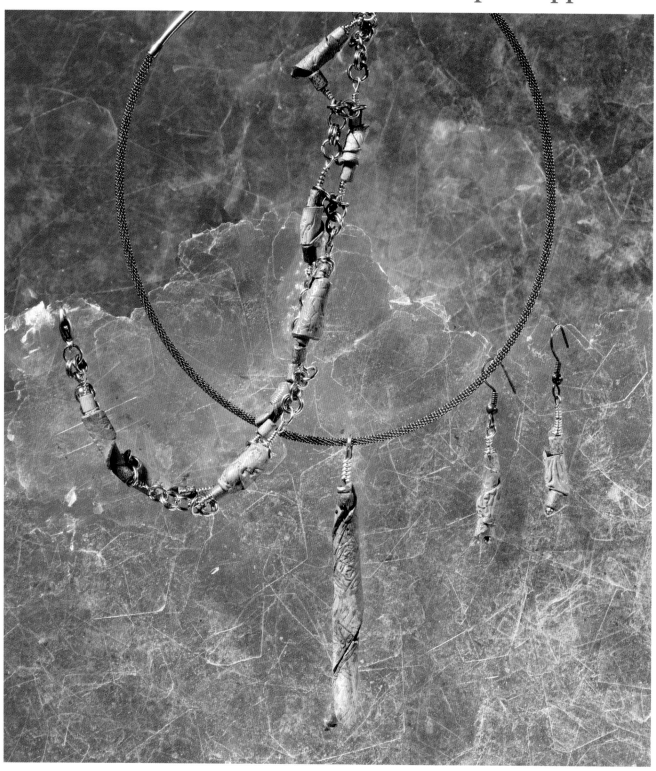

Prepare all three pieces in one firing with the rolled bead technique. I prefer rolling beads with copper and bronze clays because they are so moist and easily adhere. If you use silver clay, it will need a little slip to make the connection, but the work pays off if you want to achieve a distinguished look. An abundance of jump rings keeps things connected while adding flare.

techniques

Basic metal clay work

Wirework

Balling wire

materials

Copper clay,
0.7 ounces (20 g)

Copper wire, 20 gauge,
30 inches (76.2 cm)

20 to 30 small beads,
natural color

Approximately 100 copper
jump rings, 18 gauge,
4 mm in diameter

Copper clasp

tools

Metal clay kit, page 41

Coconut carbon

Stainless steel container

Round-nose pliers

Needle-nose pliers

step by step

1 Place a 0.7 (20 g) lump of copper clay on your work surface, and roll a slab that is three playing cards thick. Stamp texture onto the clay before cutting it into small triangle shapes that will be rolled into beads. Cut eight to ten organic triangles for the bracelet, and two triangles for the earrings. For the pendant, cut a triangle approximately 3 inches (7.6 cm) at the base, and slightly shorter on the sides (photo 1).

1

2 Create beads by rolling each triangle around a small straw; start at the base of the triangle and roll towards the point (photo 2).

2

3 Dry the beads, and fire them following the clay's recommended firing schedule. After removing the beads from the kiln and cooling them, add wrapped loops to eight beads for the bracelet. Using the 20-gauge copper wire, make one wrapped loop, thread on a small commercial seed bead, then add the clay bead. Finish by adding another commercial seed bead and a wrapped loop to secure it. Repeat eight times.

draped copper trio

4 Begin to assemble the bracelet by placing a jump ring on each wrapped loop (photo 3).

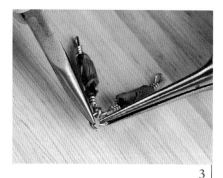

3

5 When you reach the desired bracelet length, assemble another strand of equal length. Connect the two strands of beads by attaching jump rings to all the wrapped loops, as shown in figure A, and then connect the two rows with two more jump rings.

figure a

6 Finish the bracelet by attaching a copper clasp and a jump ring to each end. Use a toggle and bar clasp if you prefer a different style.

7 To assemble the earrings, burn balls on the ends of two 3-inch (7.6 cm) pieces of 20-gauge wire. Thread a small bead on each wire, followed by the copper wrapped beads and a second small bead (figure B).

variation

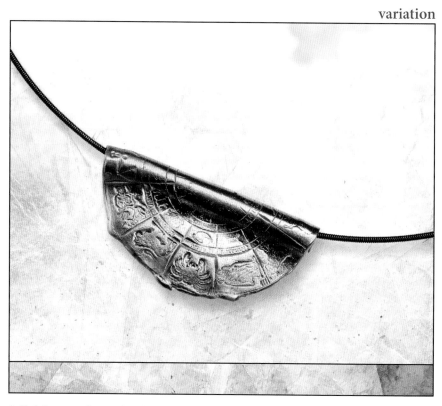

Rolled clay triangles or other shapes offer great versatility, whether you're making bracelets, earrings, or pendants. The stunning pendant shown here is simply a stamped and partially rolled copper clay circle.

8 Make a wrapped loop at the top of the earrings, and attach a commercial copper ear wire, or make your own (figure C).

9 Assemble the pendant in the same manner as the earrings. Thread a small commercial bead on a 6-inch (15.2 cm) length of wire. Then thread the large pendent bead on the wire, followed by another small bead and a wrapped loop. Finish the piece by hanging the pendant from a choker neck cord.

figure b   *figure c*

figure study

techniques
Basic metal clay work
Wirework

materials
Copper clay,
0.7 to 1.1 ounces
(20 to 30 g)
Copper
or sterling silver wire,
20 gauge, 12 to 15 inches
(30.5 to 38.1 cm)
6 to 10 silver
or copper jump rings,
4 or 5 mm in diameter
Beads for embellishment

tools
Metal clay kit, page 41
Scrap wire
Coconut carbon
Stainless steel container
Drill with 1/16-inch
(1.6 mm) bit
Needle-nose pliers
Round-nose pliers

this is one project where your creativity will soar. Figurative pendants have endless possibilities when it comes to whimsy. Multiple body shapes, special adornments, and numerous colors are just the beginning. Have fun and don't overthink it—just play.

figure study

step by step

1 If you prefer to make a pattern for the body, simply trace figure A or sketch your own on paper and cut it out. Experiment with altering the width of the arms and legs, or changing the size of the body, but remember that spontaneity works wonders.

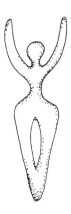

figure a

2 Place a 1.1 ounce (30 g) lump of copper clay on your work surface, and roll a slab that is three playing cards thick. Texture some of the clay with rubber stamps but leave some areas without texture. Use the craft knife to cut the figure from the clay (photo 1).

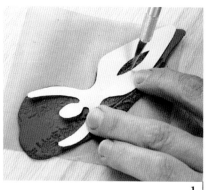

1

3 With a small piece of wire, pierce the clay in two locations where jump rings will later be connected (here, the tops of the arms are pierced) (photo 2).

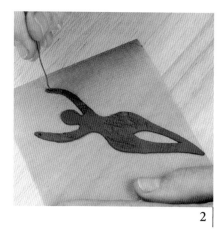

2

4 Dry the copper clay figure, then fire the piece following the clay's recommended firing schedule. After the figure is removed from the kiln, leave it completely natural, or buff the surface to bring out its shine. Make sure all the holes are open and free of carbon. If any holes closed up during firing, drill new ones in the same locations.

5 Attach jump rings through the holes. Lengthen the hanger by combining beaded wrapped loops and balled wires. Embellish the figure using wrapped loop paddles and any other wirework you find in the techniques section (page 42). I created a skirt with paddles and a necklace from a jump ring, but the options are endless.

variation

As you interpret the human form, try cutting separate clay pieces for the arms, legs, or head to make the body more flexible. Sheet metal and found objects used in conjunction with metal clay can provide wonderful personal flare.

techniques

Basic metal clay work

Balling wire

Using a ring mandrel
with clay

materials

Copper clay,
0.2 to 0.4 ounces
(5 to 10 g)

Copper
or sterling silver wire,
20 or 18 gauge,
2 to 2½ inches
(5.1 to 6.4 cm)

tools

Metal clay kit, page 41

Ring mandrel

Tapestry needle

Coconut carbon

Stainless steel container

Drill with 1/16-inch
(1.6 mm) bit

Flexible shaft drill
or scrap wire

make it chunky or delicate—either way, this handmade bead ring rolls right onto your finger. It's comfortable, stylish, and reversible.

copper ring

step by step

1 Measure your ring size, and add ½ inch (1.3 cm) to account for shrinkage of the clay. Tape a piece of nonstick surface to the ring mandrill at the appropriate size. If your ring size is 6, lay the nonstick surface at size 6½.

2 Place a 0.2-ounce (5 g) lump of copper clay on your work surface, and roll a slab that is three playing cards thick. Cut a length approximately 2½ to 3 inches (6.4 to 7.6 cm) long and ¼ to ½ inch (6 mm to 1.3 cm) wide for the ring band (photo 1).

1

3 Drape the clay band over the mandrel in a horseshoe shape and let it dry (photo 2).

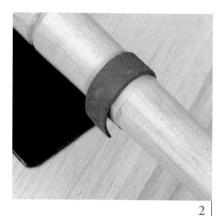

2

4 Roll a ball of copper clay between your fingers. Press it into the shape of a rectangle with rounded, thick edges. Insert the tapestry needle horizontally through the bead, creating a small hole (photo 3).

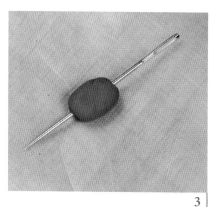

3

5 Gently stamp the bead on each side (photo 4). Dry the bead and remove the needle.

4

6 Smooth the edges of the ring band with sandpaper before firing the bead and the band at the clay's recommended firing schedule (photo 5).

5

7 After removing the pieces from the kiln and cooling them, buff them to the desired shine. With the bench grinder, buff the band's edges to make the ring smooth and comfortable to wear.

8 Try on the ring, and place the bead in the opening to determine the exact fit. Remove your finger, and drill holes on each side of the band approximately ⅛ inch (3 mm) down from the edges, or adjust the holes to your fit (figure A).

figure a

9 Check the hole in the bead to make sure it is open. If it has closed, create a new hole using a flex shaft drill or piece of wire. Burn a ball on one end of the 2- to 2½-inch (5.1 to 6.4 cm) wire. Insert the wire through one side of the band, through the bead, and through the other side of the band (figure B).

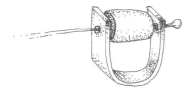

figure b

10 Burn a ball on the other side of the wire to secure the bead and finish the ring.

Using square or circular shapes for the focal bead and framing it with smaller beads can make a big difference in results.

acknowledgments

Thanks again to Lark Books for another fantastic experience. I appreciate the opportunity to once again work with a great group and produce a wonderful book.

Many sincere thanks to Marthe Le Van, Senior Editor, for her constant encouragement and ongoing support. Working with you again has been such a pleasure. The longer I know you, the more I respect your expertise and insight. You are such an amazing person, both professionally and personally.

Thanks also to Gavin Young, Assistant Editor, whose organized and efficient way of working made the editorial process a breeze. Gavin, your relaxed and easy personality made working with you a truly great experience.

It was a privilege to have the photography talents of Steve Mann and Stewart O'Shields. I am always so impressed with the images you both achieve. I have said it before, but my work always looks best when the two of you create an image of it. Special thanks to Steve for traveling to Indiana and capturing images of my studio space; it was a pleasure to get to know you.

Thanks to photography director Dana Irwin for your consistent vision of the book and to art director Megan Kirby for lending your artistic expertise. Both of you created a visually beautiful book, and I commend each of you for your talents.

Thanks to Chris Bryant for the beautiful cover design. I also appreciate the efforts of Dawn Dillingham and Julie Hale who worked on the beautiful gallery. Thank you to Nancy Wood for proofreading the book and making sure all my Ts were crossed.

Special thanks to the many talented artists who contributed their images to the gallery. It's always hard to select and edit images, and this time was even more difficult due to the exceptional work you submitted. Thank you sincerely for allowing the images of your artwork to enhance the pages of this book.

Thanks to Jackie Truty for introducing me to metal clay and encouraging me to discover all its possibilities. You have given me many opportunities to grow and learn, and I sincerely appreciate all you have done.

Thanks to Bill and Lacey Ann Struve for your persistence in the discovery and development of the bronze and copper clays. You both provided amazing support, and I appreciate your help as I discovered these two fabulous materials. Thanks to Celie Fago, whose beautiful jewelry and generous spirit have inspired me and many other jewelry artists; you are the groundbreaker.

Thanks to my friends and colleagues for the fun, laughter, and support you give me professionally and personally. Thank you again Bob for supporting me through this process and keeping the home fire burning when I am away. Thanks much to my daughter, Abbey, and son-in-law, Mac, for always being there for support and love. I appreciate you both more than you know.

Last, but definitely not least, thanks to my son, Logan, for all your help in the studio and for sharing your friends to help out. You are truly becoming an amazing young man. There is so much ahead of you, and I am thrilled to see you becoming your own person. I am proud that you are my son.

about the author

Mary Hettmansperger is a mixed-media fiber and jewelry artist with a focus on basketry, metals, and quilting. She has been teaching and exhibiting her artwork full-time for 25 years, across the United States and abroad. She teaches workshops and classes in many venues, including Arrowmont Craft School, the Bead & Button Show, Convergence, fiber and bead shops, art and craft schools, and a number of other conferences, guilds, and retreats.

Mary's work has been published in numerous books, including *Beading with Crystals, Fiber Design 7, 500 Baskets, Creative Scarecrows, Teapots: Makers & Collectors,* and *Fabulous Jewelry from Found Objects.* She is the author and illustrator of the books *Fabulous Woven Jewelry* (Lark, 2005) and *Wrap, Stitch, Fold & Rivet* (Lark, 2008). Mary has also had her work published in several magazines, including *Beadwork, Art Jewelry, Bead & Button, Shuttle Spindle & Dyepot,* and *Crafts Report.* She has appeared on several segments for the PBS television programs *Beads Baubles and Jewels* and *Quilting Arts.* Mary exhibits her work at SOFA with the Katie Gingrass Gallery and at various art shows and galleries throughout the United States.

Explore other great books by Mary Hettmansperger

Wrap, Stitch, Fold & Rivet
Making Designer Metal Jewelry
ISBN: 978-1-60059-125-9

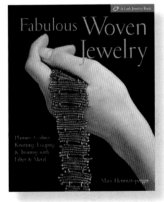

Fabulous Woven Jewelry
Plaiting, Coiling, Knotting, Looping
& Twining with Fiber & Metal
ISBN: 978-1-57990-614-6

It's all on www.larkbooks.com

Can't find the materials you need to create a project?
Search our database for craft suppliers & sources for hard-to-find materials.

Got an idea for a book? Read our book proposal guidelines and contact us.

Want to show off your work? Browse current calls for entries.

Want to know what new and exciting books we're working on? Sign up for our free e-newsletter.

Feeling crafty? Find free, downloadable project directions on the site.

Interested in learning more about the authors, designers & editors who create Lark books?

index